# Pagans, Priests, and Prophets

Books by David St. Clair
Child of the Dark
Safari
The Mighty, Mighty Amazon
Drum & Candle
The Psychic World of California
Psychic Healers
How Your Psychic Powers Can Make You Rich

# PAGANS, PRIESTS, AND PROPHETS

## A PERSONAL INVESTIGATION
## INTO THE LIVING TRADITIONS
## OF OCCULT MEXICO

# David St. Clair

Prentice-Hall, Inc., Englewood Cliffs, N.J.

For
Alejandro,
Roberto
&
Ignacio

*Pagans, Priests, and Prophets* by David St. Clair
Copyright © 1976 by David St. Clair

Printed in the United States of America

Prentice-Hall International, Inc., London
Prentice-Hall of Australia, Pty. Ltd., Sydney
Prentice-Hall of Canada, Ltd., Toronto
Prentice-Hall of India Private Ltd., New Delhi
Prentice-Hall of Japan, Inc., Tokyo
Prentice-Hall of Southeast Asia Pte. Ltd., Singapore

10 9 8 7 6 5 4 3 2 1

St. Clair, David.
    Pagans, priests, and prophets.

    Includes index.
    1. Occult sciences—Mexico.    2. Mexico—Religion.
I. Title.
BF1434.M6S24    133'.0972    76-26457
ISBN 0-13-647727-5

# Contents

Chapter 1 A Fabled and Fabulous Land 1
Chapter 2 Mexico City 18
Chapter 3 The Legends of Pre-History 39
Chapter 4 Moctezuma and Cortez 51
Chapter 5 The Virgin of Guadalupe and the Virgin
of Las Limas 63
Chapter 6 Mystical Christian Healers: Teresa Urrea,
Fidencio, and Monica Lopez 75
Chapter 7 The Pre-Columbian Tradition 92
Chapter 8 The Cult of the Dead 106
Chapter 9 The Witchcraft of the Ancients 113
Chapter 10 An Herbalist in Guadalajara 130
Chapter 11 Mayan and Huichole Shamans 149
Chapter 12 Magic Mushrooms 162
Chapter 13 The Spiritualistic Alliance 171
Chapter 14 Mary King, The Sanctuary, and El
Templo de la Fe 189
Index 213

# 1.
# A Fabled
# and Fabulous
# Land

"They shouldn't do things like that to the dead," Jorge Avila told me. "They will be punished for it. You'll see."

Jorge is seventeen and lives in the town of Guanajuato. He had seen me approaching the Municipal Cemetery, had known I was a tourist, and had asked me in rather good English if I wanted to see the mummies. "That's what I came for," I answered.

This museum must be the most macabre in the world. It stands beside the local cemetery and is run by the city. Its outside is unimpressive, its interior unforgettable.

Jorge led me past a man at the door and we walked down a white-walled corridor. Then I stopped short. Behind enormous plate glass windows were row after row of standing, seated, contorted, dead human beings whose bodies had turned to parchment. Their faces, for the most

1

part, were crying out to someone or something. Their eyes were open and their mouths formed circles of anguish against black holes or clenched yellowing teeth. Some were clothed—or rather, wearing the tatters they were buried in; others were naked. One girl, probably about twelve, stood unclothed and helpless in the middle of the room, her face frozen in fear, one hand over her breast and the other trying to cover herself between her legs. Directly behind her was a man wearing a suit and coat and a permanent grin.

In another area a woman, in a short-sleeved dress that came to her knees and whose color had long vanished, stood upright in her coffin, her bony arms crossed under her sagging breasts. At her feet was a small child, wrapped in a once-expensive red and gold cloth which was now only a rag. To the woman's right stood a large man wearing shoes, shirt, and a baggy suit. He clutched his breast and seemed to be gasping in shock, as if he had just received a bullet in his heart. On the other side of the woman, another man stood dejectedly, his arms down to his sides and his head tilted in resignation.

In another window was the severed head of what must have been an enormous man. Beside it, legs crossed almost in the lotus position, its mouth open in a silent scream, was a naked baby. A sign, in case the tourist missed the point, said "The smallest mummy in the world."

"There are one hundred and ten bodies," Jorge told me. "Sixty-three women, twenty-nine men, and eighteen babies. Some were important people here in Guanajuato. Others were just people. They came from out there." He pointed to the cemetery. "Or at least some of them did."

"Some of them *didn't*?" I asked.

"Here, you see that man over there?"

I nodded.

"You see his big moustache and see him laughing? Well, he was a Frenchman named Palazou. He lived here in Guanajuato. He had an enormous house and gave fancy parties. He had a lot of money and spent it on prostitutes

2

and good food. But he never married. When the revolution came in 1916, Palazou disappeared. His house was sacked and his fortune vanished. I mean, "Jorge laughed, "somebody got it, but who I don't know. Anyway, several years later they found his body here, among the other mummies. That was before the city took control and put them all together behind glass. They had to, you understand, because people would come by and cut the skin from the mummies to make lampshades and souvenirs. Before the city took over this place looked like a jumble of bones and skulls. You see her? The one with the long black hair? She was an opera singer. They say she was very pretty."

To understand why the mummies are not in their graves, you must realize that in most Latin countries, cemetery land is at a premium. All the deceased are buried in the Church's sacred ground, but after five years they must be dug up and their spaces given to the more recent dead. Of course, not everyone gets this shuffle treatment. If the family has the money to pay the cemetery and to keep up the grave, then the body sleeps peacefully. But in cases like that of the opera singer, nobody cared.

The mummifications were first noticed in 1905, when a grave was opened and the body removed. Instead of a pile of bones, the diggers found a perfectly preserved man, yellow and parchment-like, but a man nevertheless.

The local priest was called in to see what he thought should be done. "It would be a shame to throw these bones away," he said. "Put him in the tunnel under the chapel." And so they did. Each time an intact corpse was found, it was added to the collection. Ordinary folk who fell apart were tossed into a large pile of skulls, thighbones, and hands at the far end of the tunnel.

Authorities told me that about two percent of all the dead turn into mummies. They don't know why, but possibly it's because the earth around Guanajuato is rich in calcium. Being clay-like, it molds itself around the corpse, not letting the decomposition gasses filter out or any fresh air in.

A good theory, but what about the bodies that mummify in crypts? Above the ground, and never touching the earth?

"*Oh, no sé, Señor.*" He just didn't know.

"This is the Tlatelolco subway station," my American friend said as we drove by. "It's the first stop on Line 3, the newest of the Mexico City subway lines. And," he laughed, "this will interest *you*—it's also the area where 'the Weeping Ghost' lives."

The Weeping Ghost? It seems she appears whenever something terrible is about to happen in the area. Her apparitions are rare, but always foretell death and destruction of some kind.

The ghost is a lovely woman, about twenty-five years old, and wears a long, sweeping black dress that goes all the way to the floor. She wears a white lace ruff around her throat and smaller lace ruffs around her wrists. Her clothes go back to colonial times. So do her warnings.

The first time she was reported was in the late seventeenth century, just before terrible earthquakes and floods almost ruined the City of Mexico. The second time she was seen was just a few days before French armies invaded Mexico and put the Austrian Maximillian on the throne as Emperor. That act plunged Mexico into a civil war that took uncounted lives across the nation. The third time was in 1872, just before the death of the Great Liberator, Benito Juarez. That was the only time the disaster she predicted did not take place in the district of Tlatelolco itself.

In more modern times she appeared when the 1958 earthquake destroyed many lives and buildings in Mexico City. She was seen again in 1968 in the home of Ramón and Pilar Lopez de Pantoja. Their son, Ramón, Jr., and his American uncle, Robert Bound, were playing chess in the living room and listening to music on the stereo. The lights dimmed, the music faded away, and there she stood, dressed in black and sobbing. Young Ramón ran and awoke his father, who also came to see. All three men saw her and described her in the same way.

A few days later the world heard why she had mourned again. In the Plaza de Tres Cultures (which lies in the Tlatelolco area and was the site of the last battle between Cortez and the Aztecs), government troops opened fire against protesting university students. Tanks filled the streets, firing indiscriminately into residential apartments. Bombs were thrown, machine guns were fired, and blood ran in the streets. The Weeping Ghost had returned to warn them again.

The lady was in her early thirties and very well dressed. A large diamond and emerald ring on her finger sparkled through the iced martini glass she held in her hand. I was at a cocktail reception at the British Embassy in Mexico City and, as usually happens with me, the subject got around to the occult and psychics. "Don't get me started on *those* people!" she said in English. "I was sick for weeks because of one of them. I still become ill when I think of it." Naturally, I coaxed her into telling her story.

"When I was just a girl, I lived in a very poor farm in Guerrero State. I was one of seven children. My father died, and my mother invited a man to live with us who did the chores and took care of the crops. Soon he took not only my father's place in the fields but in his bed as well. I never really liked this man, but I obeyed him. So did my brothers and sisters. We were afraid of him because we found out that he was a witch. People would come to him and he would do things for them, you know, like hexes and curses and all that.

"Well, one day my mother became ill and we put her to bed. For five days and nights she didn't eat or drink, just lay there with her eyes open and gasping for breath. Then she died. I still remember seeing my older sister running across the field to tell me that mother was dead. Of course we were all in shock. First we had lost our father and now our mother. The only one we had to turn to was this man. He refused to let us call a priest, saying that our mother didn't want anything to do with the Church, that she had renounced the Church. We weren't too surprised, as our family had never been regular Catholics, but we did want our mother to be buried alongside our father in the Church cemetery. The man wouldn't hear of it. 'I will wash the body and dress it,' he said, 'and then we will all help bury it in the woods behind the cornfield.' After an hour or so he called us in. Mother was clean and wearing her best cotton dress. Because she had been a small woman, it was no problem for us to carry her to a hole in the forest and bury her.

"Five days later the man called us to sit at the table. It was to be a special occasion, he said, because we were to celebrate the five days that our mother had taken to get from earth into heaven. He had prepared a special soup for us and as we ate it he talked about mother and how happy she was to be among the angels. 'And she is here with us right now,' he said.

" 'How do you know?' my older brother asked.

" 'She is here on the table,' he said. 'Do you remember that I washed her body before we buried her? Well, I saved that water and made soup from it. You are being nourished by your mother right now!' "

Veracruz State lies on the Atlantic Ocean. A land of hot, palm-studded beaches and tropical rainstorms is a strange place to have leprechauns . . . except that in Veracruz, they are called *Chaneques.*

The Chaneques have been around as long as man has been there, possibly longer. The Indians told Cortez about them when he first landed on Mexican soil, and the Indians have been telling others about them ever since.

Over the centuries the Chaneques have been seen by hundreds of people. All describe them as being very small in stature, with smiling, round faces. They seem to dress in the current style because nobody has ever noted anything different about their clothes.

The Chaneques love children, whom they call "giants." They have the habit of luring a child away from its home, playing with it and feeding it, and then returning it four or five days later. The child is never harmed; on the contrary, it always returns healthy and happy.

Señora Cirila Montero Lagunes told a pair of psychic investigators from Mexico City that her son Ramiro had been saved by the Chaneques. Only three and a half years old, in March 1973 he wandered away from his home and was gone for six days. His family was frantic. The police also searched everywhere for him, but to no avail. Then the Chaneques appeared to a six-year-old neighbor boy named Juan and said to tell Señora Lagunes that her baby was in a cave ten miles away.

The police knew about that cave and went there. Sure enough, there was little Ramiro, sound asleep and happy. He told the authorities that the little people had found him along the riverbank and had taken him to this cave. They visited him all the time, played with him, and brought him food to eat. Ramiro was healthy and obviously had suffered no hunger during his six-day absence.

But the strange thing was that this cave sits several feet off the ground, on the side of a hill covered with thorns and briars. To get into the cave, the police had to cut their way up the hill and use machetes to chop away the briars. Several policemen were scratched and bleeding when they found the boy, but little Ramiro's body showed no sign of scratches or bruises. No dirt or pebbles under his fingernails, no thorns in his small hands or bare feet. Who brought him there? Who fed him and kept him warm at night?

"*Los Chaneques*," he says.

The Chaneques were also blamed for something else in 1973, but this time the mysterious results were not so pleasant. In fact, most people in Veracruz don't think it was the work of the Chaneques at all, but the doings of some beings from another planet.

Manuel Angel Gonzalez is a truck driver for the Lopez

7

Transportation Company in the town of Catemac in Veracruz State. On the morning of May 22, 1973, he was driving a six-ton truck loaded with asbestos sheetings, bags of cement, and some rods of reinforcing steel. It was a routine delivery with nothing to worry about because there was nothing flammable on board. Manuel didn't like to carry cargo that would burn. In his career he had seen too many accidents of trucks overturning and the cargo igniting before the driver could make his escape, especially in these mountain regions. But asbestos, dry cement, and steel don't burn.

He was approaching the village of Cintalapa when suddenly, ahead of him and blocking the road, were five children. He put on his brakes in a hurry, and the huge truck came to a complete stop. He started to shout at the children when he noticed they were not children at all, but men, perfectly formed but tiny. They advanced toward him, their arms in the air.

Manuel got out of the truck to have a closer look. As he did so, they came running at him. He dodged them and they shouted to him, daring him to chase them. Manuel, with that Mexican love of play, started after two of them. They led him down the side of a ravine and vanished.

Perspiring and feeling rather foolish, he climbed the hill and got back onto the highway. Then he stopped short.

His truck was engulfed in flames! Everything aboard was burning with an intense pure *blue* fire. He stood in amazement, watching the nonflammable asbestos and cement—even the steel rods—burn like rubber. Another truck pulled up and two other drivers witnessed the holocaust. In less than thirty minutes, the truck and all its contents had been reduced to ashes and rubble.

Manuel got a ride back to his trucking office and told the owner, Señor Abel Lopez, what had happened. The owner called the police, and soon the local newspaper reporters had the story. Señor Lopez said such a fire could have been caused by a short circuit in the wiring, but no ordinary fire would have consumed asbestos, cement, and steel rods.

"It was certainly something out of the ordinary," he told reporters, "and to those people who have suggested that it was deliberately set afire for the insurance, I want to say right now that this truck and its cargo were not insured. Someone also suggested that it was hit by a bolt of lightning. I don't know how that could be. It happened on a bright, clear morning."

Two days following the fire, two sections of the fused metal suddenly burst into brilliant blue flames and were reduced to ashes in seconds. The baffled police sent some of the burnt remains to the National University of Mexico and asked Dr. José de Haro Lopez, industrial engineer and professor of thermodynamics, what had caused the fire.

After extensive laboratory tests, the professor issued a statement to the press: "I must admit, I am astonished and puzzled by this case. My conclusions are that the burning of this truck and its cargo could have been caused only by an unknown type of high-heat beam with a very selective wavelength, corresponding to the laser beam but many times more powerful and not known on this planet. The combustion of the asbestos, metal, cement, and tires of the truck in such a rapid and destructive way is something I've never seen before. Almost as amazing is that the back of the plastic-covered cab seat was completely consumed, the dashboard badly burned, and the electrical wiring melted, but the bottom of the seat, the rubber floor mat, and the paint on the inside of the cab doors weren't even scorched. Even more astonishing, the fuel in the tank remained intact!"

Manuel doesn't think it was the work of the Chaneques. "They only do good things for people. I think it was done by visitors from another planet."

Space people? The day before Manuel's truck had burst into flame, three ranchers reported seeing a low-flying illuminated disc hovering over the area. Several months later, two other vehicles—a truck and a car— were also consumed in the same blue fire on highways in Veracruz. Three hours *before* his car was destroyed, the driver of the car had called the police to tell them that an oval-shaped flying saucer had followed his automobile for several miles.

Mexico has always had its share of flying saucers, but they call them OVNIs, short for *Objectos Volantes no Identificados*, or Unidentified Flying Objects.

Every now and then Mexican newspapers will carry a story of OVNIs seen above towns, found hovering in the desert, or circling around airports. Miners on their way to work in San Luis Potosí all saw a flat disc hover over the mine shaft, then spin off into the mountains. In Saltillo in Coahuila State, a group of students rushed out of school to watch a strange craft that had come out of the east and then began to circle overhead, making noises that reminded them of croaking frogs.

Four months later in the same town, two lovers were on their way to Sunday Mass, discussing their wedding plans, when they heard a sound like croaking frogs. Looking up they saw "a machine that floated about 400 meters off the ground. It was making that strange noise and was moving from north to south. Other people stopped in the street and saw it with us," claims Señor Romeo Cedillo.

"Then it made a sudden change in course and sped off rapidly. In the seven seconds or so that we watched it, we saw it was intense yellow in color. It was shaped like an arrow and it had some kind of sharp turbines on its sides. There was a kind of small rounded cabin on its top, and underneath another turbine emitted a shaky cloud of rose-colored smoke. It seemed to zig-zag in space, and I don't know of any man-made airplane that can do that."

In August of 1963, the widow Josefa Enciso heard a noise in the garden of her Torreon, Coahuila State, home. Opening the curtains, she saw a shining circle of metal. Some little men inside it were looking at her. The widow Enciso promptly fainted.

In Los Mochis, Sinaloa State, two farmers were fishing and their mule was quietly grazing when a large luminous whirling disc came down beside them. The mule went in one direction and the farmers the other. Their fish were found scattered for a mile along the trail.

On May 3, 1974, Carlos Antonio de los Santos Montiel lifted his Piper Aztec 24 single-engine plane off the runway at Zihuatenejo in Guerrero State on a return flight to Mexico City. At twenty-four, Carlos had been a registered pilot for two years with some 370 flying hours to his credit. He was working for Pelletier, S.A., a company that specializes in analysis and study of water for the government. His father is the chief mechanic of Mexicana Airlines. Carlos is both a competent mechanic and pilot.

Because bad weather had forced him to remain in Zihuatenejo the previous day, he took off at 10:30 in the morning without even waiting for breakfast. He brought the small plane up to 13,500 feet and then, when he saw that conditions were still bad, climbed to 14,500 feet. Up there the sky was blue. He decided to keep that altitude all the way to Mexico City.

Lake Tequesquitengo was a favorite landmark for him on these routine flights. In order to make visual verification of his position rather than relying solely on his instruments, he decided to lose altitude and look for the lake. But as he dipped into the cloudbank, things began to happen.

The fog obscured his view of the lake but not his view of something strange on his right side. It was an object that looked like two steel plates welded together with a round windowed bump on top. It was hovering about a foot from the surface of his wing and about five feet from his cabin. He glanced to the left and there was another of these objects positioned in the same place over his left wing.

Then a third object seemed to be heading on a collision course straight at his windshield. "I was terrified," he told the authorities later, "but instead of hitting me, it made a sudden dip and flew under the plane. I felt it scrape against

11

the bottom of the body. Then I saw that while I had been travelling at 140 miles per hour, I was now only doing 120. I tried to move to the left, hoping to scare that fellow away, but the controls wouldn't work. I frantically pushed the plane to the right but nothing happened. When I tried to lower the landing gear, hoping that would get rid of the fellow under me, it wouldn't work either."

Now thoroughly frightened, Carlos radioed the Mexico City tower shouting, "Mayday! Mayday!"—the international distress signal. "My aircraft is out of control! I have no control over it. I have three unidentified objects flying around me, one came under my aircraft and hit it. The landing gear is locked in, and the controls won't release them. My position—I am on the Radial 004 from the VOR Tequesquitengo—I am not controling the plane. Center Mexico, can you hear me?"

The Mexico City airport promised to do what they could and even called his uncle (an expert aircraft mechanic) to talk with him on the radio as he tested his controls. Airport radar picked him up and saw him being raised from 15,000 to 15,800 feet. His plane "seemed to go straight up in the air, not at an angle as a normal plane would have done." Then the object over his left wing rose, flew over the cabin, hovered an instant and joined the one over the right wing. Then both flew off together toward Popocatepetl volcano.

Carlos tried the controls again. They were working perfectly. He landed with no incident.

The young pilot was examined by medical doctors and psychiatrists who said he possibly had been hallucinating because he hadn't had any food that morning or because he might have had an oxygen shortage. They said his saucer sightings were mental.

The airport authorities disagreed with the doctors. Senor Julio Cesar Interian Diaz, the Mexico City International Airport Terminal Radar Controller, said that the blip of Carlo's plane was picked up on his radar screen 43 miles away from the airport and it was the only one in the area at that time. "There was the registration of another blip which seemed to separate from Carlo's plane and move in another direction," he said. "It executed a 270-degree turn in a radius of three or four miles at a speed of 500 nautical miles per hour. I don't know of any normal aircraft which is capable of such a maneuver."

Ramiro Garza and Jorge Reichert Brawer are founders of something called C.E.F.E.E.E.A.C., which translates into "The Investigating Center for Extraterrestial Space-craft and Unusual Phenomena, Private Association." They have set themselves up as a center for all UFO (or OVNI) reports and their study. They have documents, tapes, and photographs of many flying saucers over Mexico.

One area of the country that interests these two young men is called "The Zone of Silence" in the northern town of Ceballos in Durango State, some 425 miles from the Texas border. It is a desert region that has attracted many tourists and scientists, as well as the United States government's space project people. It seems that all sounds are cut off around Ceballos, and a strange silence hovers over the area.

Dr. Richard Downs of NASA explains that in some regions of the earth, the rotation of our planet produces an electronic whirlwind that impedes the free production of sonic waves. This same vortex also attracts large quantities of extraterrestial meteorites.

On June 11, 1970, NASA launched a rocket from Green River, Utah. It promptly went off course and headed directly for Ceballos. Our army went in, recovered the nose cone, and took out several steel drums filled with sand from the area.

Mexican OVNI specialists wonder what went wrong with this rocket to make it "accidentally" land in Ceballos. They argue that if NASA can put men on the moon three times in a row, why can't they send an ordinary rocket where they want it? And why, they ask, was it necessary for Dr. Wernher Von Braun to come looking for this rocket along with the army? Can it be, they ask, that

Ceballos was an ancient base for interplanetary vehicles? Can it be that this was the only way NASA could get close to examine its soil content and its sound waves?

Before the tourist starts to laugh at the idea of ancient space people leaving regularly from Ceballos, the Mexicans quickly point out that their history—their ancient history—is filled with references to flying saucers and spacemen. They point proudly to the legend of Quetzalcoatl who said he came from another star to help the men of the world and who left Mexico consumed in fire and noise and rose into the sky on something sounding very much like a modern spacecraft.

As I traveled and talked and questioned, interviewed and doubted and listened, I was constantly amazed at the extent of psychic and occult happenings in this fabulous and fabled land. It seemed that everyone was a believer, on one level or another; everyone had had a paranormal experience. There was no holding back when they spoke of a healing they had witnessed or, better still, of a healing they themselves had had. They admitted going to mediums, admitted having their cards read, confessed their beliefs in the medals and amulets they wore around their necks. They believed in witchcraft and the evil eye. Everyone took the world of spirits to be as real and "normal" as the material world they lived in. There was no shame in recounting stories of departed souls returning.

Señora Lavinia Hernandez awoke with a sudden start. There was someone in the bedroom. She knew it. She saw a figure move toward her. Quickly she reached for the bedside lamp and turned it on.

She was alone. She scolded herself for letting this nightmare upset her in the same way every night. This was the fifth night in a row that she had had the impression that someone was in the room, trying to talk to her.

Her husband had put it down to the financial problems they were experiencing. They hadn't been in this house in

14

the city of Guadalajara for more than three months when, crossing the street, he fell and was hit by a car. He was not severely injured, but it cost him his job in the canning factory; and with no money coming in, his wife had to look for work. She found a position as a shoe clerk (she didn't have the experience for anything else), but it barely paid the food bill. Then, on top of everything, her mother passed away, and they had to pay for her funeral in far-off Zacatecas. Her mother had once been a ravishing beauty who had married three husbands. But as the years passed, her beauty passed and she became a recluse, living in a small rented home and seeing no one. Lavinia was her only surviving daughter.

Her husband didn't want to say it aloud, but he thought Lavinia's dreams arose from a guilty conscience. It had been years since mother and daughter had seen one another. Lavinia had tried, but the old lady had shut the world away. When the news came of her mother's passing, Lavinia couldn't cry. She said she couldn't shed tears for someone who never asked for love. Yet the funeral and its expenses, coming so soon after her husband's accident, had upset her more than she realized. She didn't blame herself or her mother; like most Mexicans, she blamed life and was sure this had been her "fate."

The next night she was so exhausted from the store and from her housework that she fell into bed and entered a dreamless sleep. Even the cars and trucks going by the house failed to disturb her. But there was an odor in the room and it soon reached her sleeping face. It swirled around her eyes and nose, lingering long enough for Lavinia to fill her lungs with it.

She sat bolt upright. Instantly her mind was clear. No doubting it, that scent, that sweetness, was her mother's favorite perfume. As a child she had sniffed the fancy bottles on her mother's dressing table, and now this childhood fragrance was back with all its original intensity. She stared around her, her eyes searching the darkness of the bedroom. Then she saw the figure. It came out of the far wall and walked toward the bed.

15

Almost as a reflexive action Lavinia reached for the lamp, but her hand hit it too sharply, knocking it to the floor. She wanted to scream and wake her husband in the next room, but while her mouth would open, the sounds would not come out.

The figure came nearer. She sucked in her breath because now, forming out of the mists, was her mother's face! It was the face of the beauty she remembered as a child, the incredibly large brown eyes and the silken black hair. She saw the gold earrings sparkling with seven diamonds that had been her first husband's gift. She could see, hanging from the ghostly white neck, the diamond necklace that her second husband—Lavinia's father—had given her. The apparition raised its hands, sparkling with diamond rings. Cupped in them, and pointed toward Lavinia, were three solid gold bracelets and one of silver encrusted with emeralds. Lavinia remembered those jewels, of course, but she also remembered her mother telling her that over the years, she had sold the items one by one to pay her expenses. The jewels had been the first to go, she knew; afterward the family home. Lavinia had been glad there had been enough money from the sale of the home so that she and her husband hadn't had to support her mother in her old age.

"You have problems, my daughter," the spirit seemed to say. Yet Lavinia didn't see its mouth open nor actually hear the words. She just *seemed* to hear them.

"You have problems. I should have helped you before this, but I was too selfish. I only could think of myself. I was foolish and I made you suffer. I'm sorry."

"No, Mother!" Lavinia cried out. "You didn't make me suffer! I loved you and you refused me. Yes, that made me sad, but I didn't suffer. I knew you had your reasons and I respected those reasons." Without wondering why, Lavinia lost all fear of this apparition. She was overjoyed to be talking with her mother again after all those years. "I loved you, Mother. Really I did! I loved you!"

The softly whirling cloud came closer. The young face

16

inside it bent over Lavinia's face, and the living woman received a kiss from the dead woman. The scent of the perfume was overpowering. Lavinia closed her eyes and smiled. She knew it was only a dream, yet it was a happy dream—a great change from the previous nightmares. She opened her eyes. The misty figure was gone. The scent was gone. She was alone. Lavinia smiled to herself, rolled over, and went back to sleep.

In the morning, on the floor beside the fallen lamp, was a pair of golden earrings with seven diamonds. Also a diamond necklace, five diamond rings, two gold bracelets and one silver bracelet studded with emeralds.

"I couldn't believe it," Señora Hernandez told me. "My mother's jewels were there! For *me*! Don't ask me where they came from. All I can tell you is that *she* brought them. I know you're going to laugh, but somehow she came back from the grave and gave me her jewels. It was a beautiful thing to do. Of course, they saved us financially. I was able to sell them, pay the hospital bills, and buy this house we are in."

She rose to get a small box on a shelf. "This is the only thing we didn't sell." She opened the box, and inside was a solid gold bracelet. "Pick it up," she told me. "Hold it. Tell me what you feel."

I put it in my hand. "Why, it's warm," I said in a surprised voice. "It's as warm as if someone had just been wearing it."

"I know," she smiled. And it was the mysterious smile that I would see all across psychic Mexico.

# 2.
# Mexico
# City

Mexico City has always been the center of Mexican life and culture. It is the capital of the country. The major industries are there, the important politicians are there, the tourists spend most of their money there, and the psychic scene is more active there than anywhere in the nation.

One would thing that because of all its modernity, subways and skyscrapers, and its sophistication, that Mexico City would have abandoned all its occult habits years ago. In fact, just the opposite has happened. Belief in things metaphysical has never been more intense than right now.

My first week in Mexico City proved this. I had been invited to a dinner party given by three young men considered tops in their professions in Mexico. One was a master chef at one of the most elegant restaurants in the city, another was a highly respected researcher at a large museum, and the third was a businessman who controls a large section of Mexico's dairy industry. Their guests were just slightly less important than they were. Cocktails were served in the well appointed living room. The draperies were drawn to shut out the noise of the traffic on nearby Avenida Paseo de la Reforma, the most important and most sophisticated street in Mexico. While Spanish predominated, other languages such as French, German, Russian, and English could be heard. Since the party was more or less in my honor, a large group of people were clustered around me politely inquiring about my reason for being in Mexico. When I told them that I was there to do a book on the Mexican psychic scene, several of them laughed.

"You won't find anything *here*," one well dressed woman said. "Possibly in the mountains, but not here."

"No," added a gentleman who worked for a foreign consulate, "the superstitions of the country have long been absent from the city. This *is* the nation's capital, you know."

I nodded. "But it seems to me," I ventured, "that there should be some remnants of these beliefs here in the city. Possibly with the working classes or the maids."

There was a murmur of assent. "Well," spoke up the well coifed lady, "I *did* have a maid who was doing funny things in her room like burning candles and some cheap powder. The poor thing," she laughed, "told me that she was trying to contact her lost brother! Can you imagine? It seems that when they were small children, she was separated from the rest of the family by an aunt who stole her and brought her to the capital. The aunt was childless and figured there would be no harm in doing what she did. Then the aunt was killed in a bus accident, and the girl was put into one of those awful orphanages. Finally, when she was twelve they let her take a job as a domestic. She worked for several families before she came to me."

"Did she know where her family came from?" I asked.

"Somewhere above Guadalajara was all she knew. And she wasn't even sure of her last name. Not that it mattered much," she laughed, "all those Indians seem to have the same last name anyway."

"She thought she could find her family after all those years?" the diplomat asked.

"Well, she kept burning that powder and those candles and I'd hear her chanting some kind of moaning song in her room at night. I'll tell you, it almost drove me crazy. Then one day—and you're not going to believe this—one day there was a knock on the door. A young man was selling some kind of floor-cleaning service, or something. I told him I wasn't interested, but the maid gave him a cup of coffee and got him in conversation. Suddenly there was a scream from the kitchen. I went running in there thinking the man was killing her but instead saw them laughing and crying and embracing. Well, and I told you you wouldn't believe this," she said, taking another sip of her scotch, "but that young salesman was her long-lost brother! He had been in Mexico City for about a month, had tried to get a steady job but ended up selling that floor-cleaning stuff. That day was his first day on the job. His boss had driven him to my neighborhood, had pointed at my home telling him to begin there. During the conversation over the coffee, the maid had discovered that he was her brother. Now isn't that the strangest thing you ever heard?"

There were murmers of agreement and surprise. "But you said this maid *did* work for you," I said. "Doesn't she any more?"

"Good Heavens no! I fired her immediately! I don't want someone in my house who knows how to do those things! Imagine what she could do to *me* if she had a mind to! Anyway, those things frighten me."

"Then you *do* believe?" I questioned.

"Well . . . yes . . . I suppose I do. I mean I *know* there are things out there that I can't control, but some people *can*. That frightens me. I'd rather not have it in my home, thank you."

I searched the faces of the others. They were deciding whether or not to add to the conversation. "You know I don't really believe in these things," the diplomat finally said, "but a couple of months ago a funny incident that I can't explain occurred at the consulate. The consul's wife had lost a diamond clip after a dinner party one night and was quite upset about it. It had been a gift from the president of her country. She searched everywhere, in her home, the car, and even in the office thinking she might have lost it there. She asked the hostess who had invited her to dinner that night if she had found the clip. She remembered putting it on at home, driving to the consulate, picking up her husband, and then going on to the dinner. When she arrived home the clip was missing.

"For three weeks the poor lady looked and worried, then one day a Mexican friend gave her the name and address of an old man who lives out near the airport. He is supposed to have magic powers to find lost objects. She was so desperate that she went to see this man. She told me that all he did was throw a few sticks on the ground and sprinkle her hands with some sweet-smelling water. Then he told her not to worry, that the clip would be found in four days. She was furious that she had driven all the way out there and had paid this man—in advance—for this nonsense. She said she was more furious with herself than with him, for she should have known better. Anyway, four days later she went into her bedroom, and there was the clip right in the center of her bed! Just sitting there!"

"But her maid must have stolen the clip and put it there out of fear," a man spoke up.

"Impossible," the diplomat replied. "The maid worked only half a day that day because she had to go to a wedding. She cleaned the bedroom, put everything in order and then left. The lady of the house had been in and out of the bedroom several times that afternoon, and at one time she even sat on the edge of the bed to make a phone call. No, nobody came into that bedroom. The diamond clip appeared all by itself!"

After that the conversational theme was firmly established, and everyone insisted on telling a story that had happened to him or to someone close to him.

During my last month in Mexico I was invited into the home of one of *the* top families in the nation. I have given my word that I would not use their real names. It might cause political embarrassment for a few that were there that evening.

Their home is in San Angel, which is the Beverly Hills of Mexico City. It takes more than just money to buy a home there, and the house where I had been invited to dinner took up an entire city block. To get in, I had to ring the bell at an iron gate and then walk for at least five minutes through a private park before reaching the lavish reception hall that led into an enormous and richly appointed living room. Dinner was served in the dining room from silver trays by two butlers with white gloves. The conversation touched on politics, the world economy, the latest drama presentation in Mexico City, and painting. It became lively only when I mentioned the reason for my trip to their city.

Instantly everyone at the table wanted to tell of his personal psychic experiences. We finished the dessert hearing about a telephone call that had awakened a lady from a sound sleep to warn her of an impending danger. The voice on the other end of the line had been her mother's. But her mother had been dead for seven years.

We retired to the library while cognac and brandy were served. While some of us continued to discuss the supernatural, others talked of business, politics, and social gossip.

All conversation abruptly ceased and all eyes looked upward at the sound of solid footsteps walking on an open wooden balcony that ran around the room some twenty feet up. It was built to give access to the books nearest the ceiling. We all looked, but didn't see anyone. There was speculation about who it might be, and the lady of the house decided it must be her father. It wasn't the first time these footsteps had been heard in the library, she said.

Several minutes later footsteps came again. Again all talk stopped as everyone's eyes searched the vacant second-floor walkway. "Yes," said the hostess, "I'm positive it is my father. He loves this room and enjoys friends and stimulating conversation."

One lady there that evening had not been all that interested in the subject of the occult and once, during dinner, had flatly denied that there were such things as spirits and supernatural forces. She never had anything happen to *her*, she claimed, and wouldn't believe any of it until something did. After the second set of footsteps (which she *did* hear) she rose from her place on the sofa and came over to where I was in conversation with an eminent Mexican psychiatrist who was telling me he sometimes used psychic means to cure his patients. She stopped about two feet from me and opened her mouth to say something when suddenly she leaned backward and fell with a thud onto the thick Persian carpet.

Everyone ran to her aid, but she got up unhurt. There was a terrified look in her eyes. "I didn't lose my balance," she said in a bewildered voice. "I was *pushed*! I felt two hands on my shoulders, and they pushed me off my feet! If that was your father," she said turning to the distraught hostess, "you can tell him to stop. I believe now. I really believe!"

The Mexican Association of Parapsychological Investigations (A.M.I.P.) held an international symposium together with the Association of Professors and Investigators of the Ibero-American University of Mexico City (A.P.I.) in December 1974. Over six days they discussed such topics as Kirlian photography, psychokinesis, telepathy, poltergeists, the history of parapsychology, and the medical implications of metaphysics. Such internationally noted names as Dr. Hubert Larcher, Dr. Robert Tocquet, Dr. Robert Amadou, Dr. Marcel Martiny, and Madame Yvonne Duplessy of Paris were there, along with Dr. Hans Bender of Germany, Dr. Jules Eisenbud of the University of Colorado, Dr. van der Castle of the University of Virginia, and Dr. William Roll of Duke University in the United States. The three Mexican authorities were Dr. Salvador Garcia Doreste, Dr. Carlos Trevino Becerra, and Dr. Juan M. Sanchez Perez. The sessions were well attended, and those who were there had nothing but praise for the symposium. It was the first time psychic phenomena had been given scientific sanction in Mexico.

Aside from the A.M.I.P. and the A.P.I. there are other psychic organizations in Mexico City—dozens of Spiritualist churches, for example, as well as the Hare Khrishna and Transcendental Meditation people, a Sufi group, the Mexican Association of the Friends of Tibet, the Sai Baba people, and more yoga instructors than you can shake a tortilla at.

There are even a couple of Churches of Satan, founded along the lines of Anton Le Vey's group in San Francisco. If one can believe the sensationalist press, these churches hold regular "black masses" in which the altar is a naked girl, the chalice is a skull, the hosts have been dyed black, and the wine is chicken blood. The candles are as black as the priests' vestments and the incense during the ceremony is burning marijuana. Their "Lord's Prayer" begins "Our father who *was* in heaven," referring to Satan before he was thrown out of paradise. Of course, the majority of Mexicans want nothing to do with this "sacrilegious blasphemy."

It is written on the inside of the temple:

"Nobody knows, nobody can imagine,
  The mysteries
  Of Leonardo Alcala'
  King of Kings."

Leonardo Alcala? King of Kings? Who was this man that everyone talks about? And who is this First Lady of the World? Who is Maria Engracia?

It is number 32 on that quiet street known as Canal del Norte which runs through a quiet Mexico City working-class

24

neighborhood. To differentiate this structure from the others, there is a sign: "General Office of the Kingdom." The door is always open. After all, this is a temple, a place of worship, and as such, should not be closed to the faithful.

I go in and stop to read some of the hand-lettered signs that line the lobby: "Your life is not your own. I can take it from you when I wish." "He who laughs at this place will be punished." "Pity on him who wishes to scorn me because he will fall insensible." "A woman should dress honestly; her skirt should come down to her calves."

I tell the young lady who comes forward that no, I haven't come for some spiritual powders but rather to interview "The First Lady of the World." I have an appointment.

I am early, I'm told. Would I have a seat? I sit, and when the girl disappears down the hall, I get up and look inside the temple. It's dark in there and difficult to tell just how many of the faithful can be seated for a service. The only lights are those from several candelabras whose candles illuminate a large oil portrait of a man wearing a black tunic and a large smile. His face is lined, his black eyes shine from out of a halo of long white curly hair that falls to his shoulders. A red ribbon runs diagonally across his chest. On it is written "Leonardo Alcala, King of Kings."

I had done some homework before I came here. I had dug into the files of Mexican newspapers and asked a few questions of oldtimers in Mexico City. What I had managed to piece together was that somewhere back around 1940 or '41, Leonardo came to the capital city from the northern state of Jalisco. He was a self-ordained minister and a self-proclaimed prophet. He had been given instructions from the Lord that he and he alone could save the Mexicans from eternal damnation.

It hadn't been easy to establish his headquarters in a city dominated by the Catholic Church. Few wanted to be seen with a man who wore a long robe covered with symbols of the sun and the moon and whose long sleeves and wide hem were embroidered with silver stars. He didn't ask anyone for money; all he asked was the right to set up a place of worship, and the one to be worshiped was himself.

"I am the son of God," he told a reporter at that time. "God Himself revealed this to me. It was in 1940. I was asleep and He awakened me to tell me that I had received the Holy Spirit. Then He revealed everything to me. He even gave me a gift of a special radio set so I could remain in constant spiritual communication with the people of heaven."

They were also to call him several titles, among which was "The King of Kings," "The Teacher of Teachers," and "The God of the Gods."

"I can cure any illness," he said. "I can make any trouble vanish. I can raise the dead. I can destroy the living. I can do anything because I have been given the power. My empire is the strongest of all empires. It is unique in the history of the world. Its duration will be for two thousand years. Every man on earth will someday acknowledge my kingdom."

After the right amount of publicity and some spectacular healing services, the poor and the desperate flocked to him. He was able to buy the building his "temple" was in and to enlarge it considerably. The money flowed in, but he never seemed to spend it. He remained thin and ascetic-looking, and the only luxury he permitted himself was an automobile and a driver. His voice was soft; he had a ready smile. The only time he wasn't smiling was when he was predicting the end of the world.

"The world must know," he said in 1946, "that within a few days the entire universe must obey me or suffer the consequences. The end of the world is almost upon us! A terrible universal deluge is about to wipe all humanity from the face of the earth. Only those children of Israel and those who follow me will be saved. The only true way to become my follower is to read the 'Twenty-two Precepts.' "

These twenty-two rules were supposed to have come directly to him via the special radio hook-up he had with God. Moses had to carry down heavy stone tablets; Leonardo just switched on his transistor. The precepts are printed and handed out to anyone who wishes to read them. The preface goes like this:

*The God Leonardo says: I am God. I cure all the incurable illnesses, be they spiritual or material. I was born only for you in this third era. The first era was for Moses. The second era for Jesus Christ. The third is mine.*

*Thus speaks Alcala: Those who wish to see God, here is the secret. Learn the Twenty-two Precepts until you can recite them from memory. Learn my prayer and recite it from memory. Those who do not know my precepts and my prayer will not be saved. That is the Law. In the name of the Father and the Son and the Holy Ghost, I am carrying out my Holy and Divine wishes.*

The Twenty-two Precepts seem to be an extension of the Ten Commandments, beginning with "Love God before anything else" and ending with "Do not take up arms against your brother." Sandwiched in between are admonishments against taking your brother's wife, borrowing your neighbor's property, drinking intoxicating beverages, teaching vices to your children, having abortions, gossiping, avoiding those with horrible physical deformations, and getting into wars.

In 1972 the King of Kings and the Teacher of Teachers died. His funeral was the biggest the quiet neighborhood had ever seen. Four hearses and a delegation of important people in important-looking cars followed the thin, worn-out body to the cemetery. If this man was really who he said he was, I wondered, why did he have to die?

There is a shuffling noise and a medium-sized woman with white hair and a lined face stands beside me. She is wearing a long grey robe with some sort of amulet on a gold chain around her neck. I know instantly that this is the First Lady of the World, María Engracia, who had been given control of the temple when the King of Kings went to his resting place.

"Hail in the name of God Leonardo, King of Kings, Teacher of Teachers, God of the third era and Son of the Eternal Father," she says in a voice that seems to come from somewhere deep inside her.

"Hail," I reply, thinking that a simple *buenos tardes* would not be sufficient after a greeting like that. "Are you The First Lady of the World?"

"I am. And you are a writer?"

"I am."

"There is nothing I can tell you that you will not discover for yourself if you read and memorize the Twenty-two Precepts. Once you understand them and recite them, then you will see the God Leonardo personally and can talk to him and ask him whatever you wish. You will see him in all his glory as he sits at his rightful side of his Father the Eternal God of Creation."

"But I really don't have time to do all that," I explain. "I'm in rather a hurry."

"The King of Kings took years to allow a tiny seed to become a giant tree. If he could take the time, so can you." She turns to go. "You will excuse me now."

"Just a moment, please, Señora. May I ask you a question about you? I'm sure I won't find the answers in the Twenty-two Precepts."

She turns toward me. "I have no past, and my future is with my King someday. Before I met him I was a mortal sinner suffering from all the sins and pains of the human race. I was desperately ill and none of the doctors that I consulted could help me. When I heard about Leonardo, I came to him at once. You may say I was guided to him. He put his hands on me and my illness vanished. I stayed on to become his assistant and now to become his living symbol on earth."

"But you are now a healer yourself, aren't you?" I ask.

"I along with others in the temple have been given the power to heal any illness, yes."

I had heard of the healings here, plus the special ointments, incense, candles, and holy water that could be had for a price. Again she turns to go.

"Please just one more question," I insist. "Why did the God of Gods have to die? Why wasn't he immortal?"

She sighs. She has probably had to answer this question a thousand times since her God's funeral. "It was written that the Teacher would someday take his place beside the Eternal Father."

"And you are carrying on his work?"

"I and the faithful do not worry about his passing or the work that must be done. You see, young man, he has returned in spirit and is always here with me. He gives the instructions and I carry them out. Now that his mortal body is gone, he is freer to do more things for more people in more places. I see him every day, constantly."

"And the others," I ask, "do they see him too, or is it just you?"

"I cannot give you any more information," she says. "Too much has already been printed that is false and injurious to the King. He has forbidden me to talk about himself to others. Therefore you will excuse me." It is not a question, it is a statement, and she goes into a room off the altar and closes the door. I glance up at the portrait. The smile seems to be gone and in its place a thin-lipped scowl. Aimed at me? I don't bother to think twice about it but walk quickly out into the warm Mexican afternoon, where the honking cars and the screaming children restore my rapidly fleeing sanity.

Magic as a way of life is nothing new to the Mexicans. They've heard about it all their lives, have seen it in practice. Although the fair faces and the blonde hair in the cities might belie it at first glance, most Mexicans have Indian blood in them. Those who have European blood will tell you about that part of their family tree first, proud that it gives them social standing apart from their maids and houseboys.

A young lawyer in the city of Puebla defies the local image of a lawyer by wearing sport shirts to the office and leaving them unbuttoned to show off his hairy chest. "Because of my dark skin and my dark eyes," he told me, "I must prove to my wealthy clients that I am not an Indian. These chest hairs are proof that I have Spanish blood in my veins. Did you ever see a hairy Indian?"

The class struggle has been going on since the revolution of 1919, but supposedly democratic Mexico is democratic only on paper. City people still get the lion's share of government services. Paved streets, electricity, running water, and schools are for those communities who have the political clout and the money to pay for them. The lighter the skin and the blonder the hair, the better chance one has of becoming a general in the armed forces. In business, a blonde who can't take dictation will probably get the secretarial position that a dark-skinned girl could fill just as well. Magazine and television advertisements for such articles as cigarettes, beer, and cosmetics almost always feature an attractive blonde. When they are trying to sell canned soup, floor wax, and detergent, they'll show a dark-skinned girl.

Surnames aren't any way of telling if a person is "society" or not, because even the lowest Indian can have a name like Lopez or Garcia. If you want to be recognized in Mexican upper circles, the thing to do is to accumulate as many names as possible and then use them all. Juan Jorge Martinez Mendoza de Palmas is obviously a more important person than Juan Palmas. A medical doctor I met in Mexico City confessed that when he changed his name from Luis Gomez to Rudolfo Livshinsky his clientele doubled, thinking they were in the care of a European-born medical man. Class lines are carefully drawn in Mexico, and it is difficult for an Indian to step across them. Not even if he has lots of money can he be sure of acceptance by the Mexicans.

Yet when it comes to the psychic side of Mexico, class lines are ignored, skin color overlooked. Family background means nothing. The world of spirit is a great leveler, and many of the top mediums and psychics in Mexico today are Indian rather than Mexican.

The Mexicans believe that the best psychics and witches are "in the country," hidden in small villages that are themselves hidden in rocky mountain passes or in thick jungle vegetation. They believe that the power of the uneducated and unsophisticated villager is greater than that of any city dweller, that the peasant is more "in tune" with the natural forces. White-skinned, hairy-chested clients travel for miles to consult with hairless, dark-skinned witches and clairvoyants. I met a Mexico City couple, both with college degrees, who spend one week of their annual vacation driving to a small town in Oaxaca State and then walking for three miles up the side of a mountain to consult with an old woman who "is just fantastic about what she knows about us!"

A society matron in Mexico City brought a medium from a small village straight to her home and installed her as "maid in charge of polishing the silver." The old lady sits in a back bedroom and occasionally wipes a cloth over a tarnished teapot, but her main occupation is to advise the matron on her every move. When guests have had their dinner, the "silver polisher" will give them individual readings. While the other maids look upon this old crone with anger, they don't dare complain for fear of getting a curse put on them. I had a reading with the old lady myself. She turned out to be a marvelous fraud, but the matron accepts every word she says as gospel.

If you want to find a witch or a medium or even a healer in Mexico City, you'll have a bit of trouble until you can be oriented by someone who has lived there and who knows the ropes. Not so if you want your cards read, however. The "Café Turco" places are all over town. The only problem is knowing which are the best ones. "Café turco" means Turkish coffee, and it is in these coffee houses where the Tarot readers dwell. Some establishments have names like "Sun and Moon" or "Abracadabra" or "Zodiac," but the best one seems to be a rather unpretentious little place called Café Khrishna on Calle Oslo in the heart of the fashionable Zona Rosa. It's a small place with Indian murals on the walls. You can have a sweet roll and a café turco—or a café americano—at one of the eight tables. The place will hold twenty customers at full capacity, and it's usually full—thanks to its owner Gustavo, the best card reader in Mexico City.

Gustavo must have another name, but he refuses to give it. He says having just a first name is easier for his clients to remember and sounds more professional. He is somewhere in his late twenties, short, with dark skin and piercing dark eyes. He wears a full black curly beard that gives him a ferocious appearance. His soft voice and flashing smile remove that impression quickly, however.

I had inquired of several people in the psychic field about a good Tarot card reader, and all of them said "Gustavo" right off the top. He was more than willing to be interviewed and more than willing to help me with my other research. Thanks to him, I was able to get a deeper insight into Mexican occultism than I ever could have done on my own.

Gustavo speaks English as softly as he speaks Spanish, which makes his clients and friends pay attention to every word he utters. He was born in Mexico City and is one of eight children. His father has been employed (in an important position) in the American Embassy for over twenty years. He wasn't too happy when Gustavo graduated from the University and became a professional card reader. His other sons had gone to college and the family had an industrial photographer, an electronics engineer, a computer technician, a professional musician, and a veterinarian. His two daughters married professional men. "My father should have seen it coming all along," Gustavo says, "for my mother's side of the family is loaded with psychics."

His uncle, Milton Arauz, is a well-known medium and

healer. When Gustavo wasn't going to spirit sessions and healing services with his mother, he was over at his uncle's learning about Tarot cards. Like medium Peter Hurkos of Holland, he fell on his head from a second-story window. It happened when he was twelve. He says he felt a pair of invisible arms grab him just before he landed on the cement patio. "There was no pain, no concussion, nothing. After that I knew I was protected. I understood that what my mother and uncle had been telling me was true. So I started looking into my life to see why I deserved this special protection."

After several sessions with his uncle, he gave his first "professional" reading. "I was only thirteen and the client was a friend of my uncle's. He knew her well, but I had never met her. I charged her twenty centavos. Not because I needed the money, but my uncle taught me the professional ethics. One must always receive something for a reading, even if it's only a token payment like twenty centavos. I was very nervous as I put the cards out on the table, and to my horror she didn't agree with anything I said. I thought it was because it was the first time I'd tried it with anyone. I didn't know anything about her; I was only telling her what the cards told me. Finally she said, 'Young man, I can't agree with anything you've told me. I'm afraid I'm wasting your time.' And she left the room.

"I was heartbroken, but my uncle only laughed. 'I know that woman very well,' he told me, 'and everything you read for her was the truth. She is one of those people who never admit the truth about themselves. That's why I chose her for you. Congratulations. I'm proud of you.' "

I wondered if the same card always means the same for each client; if Gustavo always interprets the Tower or the Emperor the same way each time it appears.

"Oh no. It always depends on how the cards fall and what other cards are near. They never have the same meaning for everyone. A good reader, a good *interpreter,* reads the cards as to their meaning at the moment. A good interpreter never reads the cards the way the instruction sheet that comes with the deck tells him they should be read. Of course, a reader must learn a basic technique, but that technique must be constantly changing and developing with the more experience he acquires and with each new client he has. Even if a client has a problem similar to that of the client who was there just before him, you can't interpret the cards in the same way.

"If a client says your reading is not applicable to his personal problems," I asked, "and you lay the cards again, would they come out exactly the same the second time?"

"That's only happened to me three times in my life," he said. "Often a person does not want to accept the interpretation because he does not want to believe something about his life. Many people deliberately fool themselves into thinking they are different from what they really are. When that happens, I'll lay the cards again. They probably won't be in the same position as before, but the interpretation will be the same. The same *meaning* will be there the second time."

I asked him about some of his more memorable readings. He paused and ran his hand through his dark beard. "You know, I see so many people that it's difficult to know which was the *best* reading. And, too, many clients don't tell me if the reading was good or not. They just thank me and go away. When I do predictions in a reading, I hardly ever hear of the results."

"Well," I insisted, "can't you remember any *one* that stands out from the others?"

"Oh, there was this American girl who came in here one afternoon with some other tourists. I told her that soon she would go to a doctor. He would tell her she had a small growth somewhere on her body, but would say it wasn't important. I told her not to listen to that doctor, but to go immediately to another doctor and get a second opinion. She laughed and said she would do that if such a thing ever occurred. Two years later she was back in Mexico City and she came to see me. At first I didn't even remember her. She told me she had gone to a doctor in Washington, D.C. He had found a small growth on her ovary, but had told her there was nothing to worry about. She recalled my reading and went immediately to another doctor. That doctor insisted the growth be removed, and it turned out to be cancerous.

"Another time a wealthy businessman came to me for advice about his company, and I told him he would be divorced within six months. He laughed and said it was impossible, that he loved his wife and had no intention of divorcing her. Two days later his wife's lawyer presented him with divorce papers. She was in love with another man. He did not contest it, and within six months from the reading he was divorced. Because of that reading he brought his teenage daughter to see me. She was a pretty girl still wearing her high-school uniform. I told her that she would be married within four months and to a much older man. Her father called me that night and gave me a lecture, telling me my powers had certainly slipped. He was quite angry about the reading and said his daughter was making plans for college and didn't even have a boy-friend. Four months later he called me to apologize. His daughter had met a thirty-year-old man, had run off and was married."

I asked him a loaded question. "Do you really need those cards, or are they merely a form of concentration?"

He didn't hesitate in his answer. "The cards are, for me, a way of careful interpretation, a way of tuning into the sensibilities of the client. Their vast symbology covers all aspects of human life and thought. They are a vehicle for sensitivity. The designs on them contain a series of ideas and conceptions that can be translated into a person's thoughts. Of course, many times I don't need the cards, but they greatly help me to concentrate and capture something about the stranger in front of me. Many people say 'the cards are working,' but I don't think so. It's the reader who is working and using his psychic abilities to interpret and capture the thoughts of his client. The moment the client shuffles the cards and prepares them for me, he is putting his thoughts and vibrations out into the air. He comes to me because he has a problem and needs guidance. That problem is foremost on his mind when he sits across from me and cuts those cards. The cards react like a computer, and as soon as they make contact with him they go into his particular programming. I try my very best to capture these thoughts and images. At the beginning of a long day of appointments, I pray and ask my guides and the spirits for assistance in the reading so I may be of parmount help to my clients."

This was the first time he had mentioned anything like spirits. "Are these guides of yours discarnate entities, or are they spirits that have never been human?"

"When I say spirits, I mean those who guide me, and naturally I also mean God, who is the driving force behind all things both material and spiritual. I believe in discarnate entities, as you call them. I have seen spirits give messages, lift objects from tables, diagnose and cure illnesses. I have gone into trance and have delivered messages, but I don't like to do it. I prefer to remain conscious of what I'm doing and of what is going on around me. I don't feel I need that physical possession to do my work.

"I have a spirit with me always. The spirit of a very old woman. She has helped me a great deal. She is always with me in difficult moments. One time at a medium's house she came through during a session and asked me, 'Don't you know who I am? I am your protector.' I said that I had never heard of the name she was using. Then she said she had chosen me because she needed someone to pray for her, and when I still doubted her, she told me her full name and exactly where she had been buried. I had never been there, and neither had the medium who channeled the message. I made a special trip to this small town, and there was her grave with her name and dates on the stone exactly as she had said. That was great proof for me that I was indeed protected."

Earlier, when we had gone to see an ancient woman healer in Xochimilco, he had remarked to me that he read the cards differently than they were read in the United States. I asked him about that now.

"It was the technique that I learned from my uncle. I never ask questions of my clients when they come for a reading. I don't ask them to tell me their names, their occupations, their marital status, nothing. I don't want to know what problems they have or why they have come to me. I do all the talking and I tell them what the cards say about them. During the reading their problem *always* comes to the surface. They *always* get their question answered."

"That way you can't be accused of pumping them."

"Correct. There are readers who start off by asking a client his birth sign and then giving a pat astrological reading. Or else they will say, 'Your girl friend is . . . you *do* have a girl friend, right?' and from that they proceed with their reading. I don't think that a professional should *ever* converse with his clients or ask questions. The professional should *tell* the client. I know readers who watch their clients' eye movements to see in that way if they are correct and should continue on that general line. I look at the cards, almost never into the eyes of my clients."

Gustavo charges sixty-five pesos for a reading in Spanish and seventy-five if you want it in English. Most readings take anywhere from a half hour to a full hour, and his wiser clients phone for an appointment several days in advance. His day at the café begins at two in the afternoon and sometimes runs until two in the morning. He also is called into the living rooms and cabinet rooms of some of the most important personages in Mexico City. Many of his readings are for politicians in *very* high places.

"Sometimes a new client will come to me and he'll say, 'Tell me only the good things you see,' and I tell him that if he only wants the good things, he should go to another reader, not to me. If he leaves I don't care, because if he has time to listen to the good things, he has time to listen to the bad things as well. Some say I'm too honest in my readings, but I never say anything negative without looking for something positive to balance it out. Many confused people come to me and I consider it part of my mission to orient them and put them back on the right track. I have no control over their problems. *They do*. That's what I try to show them.

"I consider my work necessary. It's not just for fun. Many people have no one to turn to for advice, and here with me, for sixty-five pesos, they can get counseling and have a cup of café turco at the same time. It does not have the stigma and is much cheaper than consulting a psychiatrist."

# 3.
# The
# Legends
# of Pre-History

Mysticism among the upper classes is nothing new in Mexico. It had been going on long before the Spanish conquerors arrived and discovered that the high Aztec rulers were also true believers in the powers of the supernatural.

Quetzalcoatl was the Jesus Christ of the ancient pre-Spanish world. Some say he *was* Jesus Christ; that shortly after His crucifixion in Jerusalem, Christ appeared in what is now the United States and started preaching and instructing the tribes. He visited the Hopi nation, then started down into Mexico. The Toltecs, the most powerful group in Mexico at that time, tell of a god who came walking into their city unexpectedly one warm afternoon. He was white-skinned, had a beard, and spoke with a soft voice. What he had to say impressed them immensely—so much so that they adopted his teachings and spread them down the length of Mexico and into Central America. He taught them science and showed them how to calculate the stars. He spoke of love, of his home in the sky, and of his immortality. One day he went away, but promised to return in the year Ce Acatl, or the year 1519.

The Toltecs were so taken with this god that they constructed great pyramids in his honor. To him they built the magnificent religious area known as Teotihuacan. It was indeed a "City of the Gods." It still is.

Nothing like it exists anywhere in the world. It sits in ruined splendor some thirty miles from Mexico City and is dominated by the four-level Pyramid of the Sun that occupies a 750-square-foot base and rises 217 feet into the air. At the end of an enormous square, facing this pyramid, is the Pyramid of the Moon. It rises 149 feet and is surrounded by thirteen temples. To one side of this square sits the Citadel, enclosed in stone walls 1,300 feet long. On three sides of the square stand four pyramid-shaped bases that once housed temples. On the east side of the square are three other bases. Between the two large pyramids to the sun and moon runs the three-mile Street of the Dead with the remains of temples and palaces that once housed priests, acolytes, and high religious personalities.

In the center of it all is the Temple of Quetzalcoatl. It was his alone, in his rightful position between the sun and the moon. His religious image, a plumed snake, adorns the facade. For the man who could walk on the ground and fly like a bird, who dominated the earth and the sky, the snake symbolized the earth and the feathers the heavens. This face alternates with that of Tlaloc, the God of Rain—a natural combination, for without rain the sun could not nourish the earth. Yin and yang in the New World.

Archaeologists have claimed these buildings were erected sometime between 200 B.C. and A.D. 150. There is no doubt the pyramids came first. The Temple of Quetzalcoatl was added later. But archaeologists also agree that this great city (several thousands lived in mud and stick

houses around the plaza) was abandoned sometime between A.D. 650 and 750.

Who were the Toltecs? Nobody knows. They left no
written inscriptions, so we don't know what language they
spoke. We don't know their physical size because they
cremated their dead, and you can't very well measure
ashes. We do know that they were master craftsmen.
Nothing was impossible for their artisans. They cut stones
and left no mark. Legend says that it took four men to
carry just one of their squashes, that their corn grew so
large it was all a man could do to carry one ear at a time.
Smaller ears were used as fuel in their steambaths. They
planted cotton that did not have to be dyed; it grew naturally in colors like red, rose, yellow, violet, green, blue, and
grey-brown. It is said they knew how to cure almost every
ailment with the use of herbs. They interpreted dreams,
and were experts in astronomy.

They were a religious people. Their religion was everything to them, as can be seen by the magnificent and
majestic work that went into their great plaza. They conquered others with their religion—by peaceful means. They
traded with other tribes and spread their beliefs as they
spread their fine wares. It was almost like a Latin American Tibet with a feather-and-bead-laden Dali Lama, or a
pyramid-shaped Holy See whose pope was the direct
representative of Quetzalcoatl.

The empire spread out in physical ways as well. On the
northern gulf, at El Tajin, a splendid pyramid was built to
honor their plumed god. In the south, near Cuernavaca,
sits Xochicalco with great carvings of the plumed serpent.
And in Cholula, near the city of Puebla, stands an incredible monument to this god.

When I first saw it in 1956, it was nothing more than a
very high hill with a Catholic church perched at its very
top. Since then the Mexican government has been investigating this hill and has discovered that it is, in reality, five
pyramids, each one built directly over the previous one.
Archaeologists say the first was constructed "at the

beginning of the Christian era." Other peoples built their own temples in succeeding waves. In fact, the last pyramid was being built when Cortez and his army arrived in 1519. While it is not as high as the Pyramid of the Sun, it is broader at its base, broader in fact, than the Pyramid of Cheops in Egypt. In volume it is the largest pyramid in the world.

History is difficult enough to trace when you have all the dates at your fingertips, but with the constantly flowing tide of human invasion and conquest in Mexico, it's almost impossible to come to any real conclusions or cite specific years. We do have the records of some early Christian priests who went to Mexico to "save" it from the barbarians who had built those magnificent structures. But their information came from books the Aztecs had written (or rewritten to give themselves a better image) or from Indians at the time. Fray J. de Acosta, in a book published in 1589, says that a northern tribe called the Chichimecas came into Teotihuacan and destroyed it, sending the priests and the intellectuals into the interior and farther south. Charred beams and cinders have been found in the ruins of the great plaza. Then came the Nahuatlacas, who were composed of seven tribes and who, romantically, came from seven caves. The last of these warring nomads were the Aztecs, arriving at the long-abandoned City of the Gods in A.D. 1022.

A Catholic priest, writing two hundred years after de Acosta, reported that the Toltecs migrated from Asia in A.D. 596. Their center had been the old kingdom of Tollan. He then proceeded to list by name seven kings of the Toltecs and the dates each one reigned—quite a feat, considering that all traces of this people's history had been wiped out for over a thousand years before he began his research.

Well, where did they come from? And the others who came after them? Popular history tells us that the New World was populated by successive waves of Asians who crossed the Bering Strait and that each new flood of immigrants pushed the others farther south. With all that coming and going, that fragile point between Alaska and Russia must have looked like Grand Central Station. This supposedly happened about fifteen thousand years ago; by seven thousand years ago the immigrants had taken over the hemisphere and established centers in Mexico and Central America and others in the Andes of Peru and Bolivia. And being Asian immigrants, they all came from the same physical and cultural stock.

That theory is rapidly being consigned to the wastebasket. Recently, a stone tool was found in Mexico at Hueyatlaco, near Puebla. A Carbon-14 test indicated that it was about two hundred and fifty thousand years old! Other tools found in New York State (a long way from Alaska) date back thirty-two thousand years. Evidence has also been found to prove that thirty-five thousand years ago man dwelt around San Diego, California.

The facts today seem to agree that the New World was peopled by many different types coming from many other parts of the world, but around the same time. In my book, *The Psychic World of California,* I reported on the beliefs held by the Rosicrucians that the west coast of the United States and what is now Baja California was the last unsunken plateau of the continent of Lemuria. When the continent began to sink into the Pacific, its inhabitants went out in all directions, seeking firm land on which to begin their lives anew. They were not savages. They had their highly advanced religion. Their psychic abilities were developed to such a degree that they did not need words to communicate with one another. When they decided it was time to die, they lay down and died. They were able to "de-gravitate" stones and would fly around on them like the mythical Arabs did on their flying carpets. They knew how to release the force of gravity. To build edifices of stone was no problem: they made the stones weightless and transported a load of them like a load of feathers. They had a type of cutting tool (a prehistoric laser beam) that worked on the principle of sound. We know—with our "advanced" scientific minds—that sound waves can break a crystal goblet. The ancient Lemurians used the same idea to cut stones—or anything else for that matter—without leaving chisel marks. They could measure the exact proportion they wanted the stone to have, then slice it like butter, float it to where they wanted, lower it into place, then let gravity take over again.

If all this sounds far-fetched, consider the magnificent stone structures in the New World. Stones weighing several tons were transported from quarries miles away. If we insist in believing that these stones were carried in the traditional overland manner, then we must believe that there were hundreds and hundreds of men employed day and night cutting these stones, dragging them over mountains and across rivers, driving horses and oxen to death with these monumental loads. But there were no horses in America until Cortez brought them. The delicate llamas the Incas domesticated could never have dragged into the city of Cusco those enormous room-size boulders, many of which weigh more than twenty tons.

A few years ago the Mexican government moved a massive Olmec stone head found in the Oaxacan jungles to the Anthropology Museum in Mexico City. It took them several days to make the trip. The truck they used had to be specially reinforced before its more than thirty wheels would carry the load.

Supposedly, some of the Lemurians flew across the area known as North America and landed on the continent of Atlantis. The sinking of their original home had displaced the waters of the world to a drastic degree. As Lemuria sank, other land arose. River basins emptied and dried. Lakes lost their outlets. The Salt Lake in Utah at one time was an inland sea. The Amazon basin at one time was another. The Gulf of Mexico was at one time high and dry land.

There was a world calamity—that is certain. Whether it was a collision with another planet, as some have suggested, or the sudden shifting of the earth's axis which plunged tropical areas into snow and made mountains of ice melt into tropical rain forests is still a mystery. But water was part of the disaster. *Every* primitive culture has its version of the earth destroyed by a great flood.

We Judeo-Christians do not have a monopoly on Noah. And we have to abandon the notion that man, before he was blessed with Western knowledge, was not much more than an animal. It soothes our educated souls to think that we are now at the peak of civilization, that there has never been anybody any better than we are right now. We glory in comparing our lifestyles and that of the so-called Neanderthal man, who we think of as living in caves, eating raw meat and hitting his mate over the head with a club.

We do not stop to think that somewhere along the line something happened—around the same time—in both the northern and southern hemispheres of America and in Egypt that changed the course of mankind. In these places, there are no traces of slow evolution. *We have no signs that the Mexicans and Egyptians developed their cultures gradually.* They appear complete, with an organized religion, farming, an artistic culture, social organization, and highly sophisticated mathematical and astrological concepts.

Of course, there were Neanderthal men, Peking men, and the "African Genesis" men, but even today we have differences in social knowledge and levels of civilization. What would an archaeologist, five thousand years after nuclear war, think of the United States if he discovered the remains of the subway in New York and a mule wagon in Mississippi?

The myth of Quetzalcoatl follows the life of Jesus Christ in a most intriquing way . . . and the Catholics did not give his legend to the Indians. It began when he simply appeared one day and announced that he was one of the great gods who had been sent to teach the Toltecs all the knowledge in the world, a knowledge based on peace and love. War—and human sacrifices—were not included in his dogma. (They came later with the invading hordes from the north.) This white-skinned man with a light beard set about to change the course of the lives of these primitive peoples. In the Aztec language of Nahuatl, his name was a combination of *quetzal* (a brilliantly plumed tropical bird) and *coatl* (snake). He has other names like Twin Brother (because of his relationship to the God of the Sun), Lord of the Dead, and Lord of the Dawn. His feathered dress has come under scrutiny lately as many students begin to wonder if the feathers were not really a symbol for the fact that he came from the sky.

He ruled well but not long, because soon the evil god Tezcatlipoca (the Devil) came and tempted him. He told Quetzalcoatl he was very handsome, and when he showed the god his face in a mirror, Quetzalcoatl was very upset. It was the first time he had seen his earthly body, and he became aware of it on the carnal level.

Then this ancient devil offered him a drink of *pulque*, a potent alcoholic brew made from fermented cactus. Quetzalcoatl refused, but the devil insisted, and so Quetzalcoatl put in a finger and tasted it. He liked it, so he had a cup of it and then another cup and another. After the fifth drink, the devil sent for Quetzalcoatl's sister. She had five drinks too, and they went to bed together.

When Quetzalcoatl awoke he was ashamed to have become egotistical, gotten drunk, lost his chastity, and seduced his own sister. In other words, he had descended from his lofty position as a god and had become like a mortal man.

He ordered a stone box to be made and crawled inside it. There he stayed for four days, thinking on his destiny and what he must do. Finally he announced that he was going away. He gave all his possessions to his followers and started for the seashore. There he put on his magnificent mask of feathers and built a huge fire. He jumped into the fire and was consumed. Eight days later his heart appeared in the heavens—a star. The Indians gave it one name; we call it Venus.

The parallels are there. Like Christ he appeared from

an unknown source. He taught; he was wise and good, he was tempted by the Devil, but, unlike Christ, he gave in to the temptations. He gave away his earthly possessions, walked to his own appointed place of death, and didn't fight destruction. He died. He was reborn as a star.

But another more recent interpretation says he was one of the leaders from another planet who came to instruct the Indian world. He was wiser and technically far advanced; he "saw his body" and realized he was becoming human. When he gave in to drink and sex, he knew it was time to go, that his mission would not get any further because he was forgetting who he was. During those four days in the stone box, was he communicating with his superiors? Was the box in reality some kind of interspace radio shack? He walked to the seashore. Can it be that he had originally arrived at this seashore, where his spacecraft had landed? Remember, he appeared *walking* into the Indian city. But he put on his mask of feathers (his space suit?), was consumed in a giant fire, and vanished. Could that fire have been the propulsion that lifted him toward home? It's fascinating to think about and to romanticize, but so far it's all myth and conjecture.

At this point the Aztecs get into the act with their interpretation and stretching of the story. They told the Spanish priests accompanying Cortez that shortly after his fiery death, Quetzalcoatl appeared in what is now the Yucatan and instructed the Mayans in astronomy and religion. Probably, say the anthropologists, the fleeing Toltecs and those who came after them gave their religious beliefs and astronomical talents to the Mayans.

Astronomy was very important to the ancients of the New World. They had the courses of the major planets all detailed, with Venus-Quetzalcoatl as the major star. They worshiped this enormous ball of white fire that in their latitude comes up brilliant and awesome in the dawn sky. It was to them the personification of their great teacher-god who had made the safe journey through the under-ground of the Earth (a place of death and destruction that all Indians feared) and had arrived safely back in the sky.

The Indians of Mexico were not the only ones to venerate Venus. The Egyptians, Greeks, Chaldeans, Babylonians, and Romans assigned special significance to this planet. It gave promise of a new day, new hope. Venus is the planet nearest the Earth that also orbits the sun, and so appears before or after the sun in the dawn or evening sky. It is only slightly smaller than the Earth and reflects 76 percent of all the sunlight it receives.

But the planet was important to the ancient Mexicans for other reason than the possibility that it might be Quetzalcoatl. In fact, this planet was the reason they became such experts in astronomy. They studied it, charted it, and even set their calendar by it. Five Venusian years had 2, 919.6 days. Their lives revolved around these five-year cycles. So did their religion. Why?

Of all the ancient peoples in the Eastern Hemisphere, the Babylonians were the experts in astronomy. Three thousand years before Christ, they had only four planets in their charts: Mars, Mercury, Saturn, and Jupiter. If Venus was the brightest and nearest to the Earth, why had they not included it? Where was it? And why such significance after it appeared?

In 1950, in a brilliant book titled *Worlds in Collision,* Immanuel Velikovsky put forth his reason for Venus and its constant surveillance by the ancients. It was a theory so different from that of the scientists of his day that he was laughed at and scorned. Yet, some twenty-five years later, the laughter has died down. More has been learned about the effects of the planets on the Earth. More has been pieced together from the different ancient civilizations. More information shows that perhaps Velikovsky was right.

According to his theory, the reason the Babylonians didn't include Venus in their charts was that five thousand years ago, Venus simply did not exist. It wasn't until four thousand years ago that Venus came tearing out of the bowels of the planet Jupiter. It headed toward Earth and its pull caused havoc on our planet. Its force hauled up the waters of the seas and covered the lands. Twice in fifty-two years Venus almost hit Earth. The first time she caused the great flood of Deucalion at the time of Moses in 1516 B.C., and the second time the Flood of Ogyges at the time of Joshua in 1568 B.C. Some experts now think that it was at this time—not nine thousand years ago, but more like thirty-five hundred years ago—that Atlantis and Lemuria were overwhelmed with water and sank.

Then, according to Velikovsky, Venus remained a comet for seven hundred years, feared by all ancient people as it sped crazily around Earth. Sometime around 747 B.C. it moved nearer to Mars and caused another upheaval of water on our planet. In 687 B.C. it flooded us again, at which time Mars was pulled out of orbit and Venus's orbit became circular rather than elliptical. It stopped terrorizing Earth, settled down, and became a bright reminder of what it had been.

Velikovsky's theories are starting to be taught in colleges and universities. They are being studied now, not classified with other works of science fiction.

So it would seem that the great interest of the ancient Mexicans toward the movement of the stars was not just to find out what day it was, but to discover when the *next* catastrophe would occur. They wanted to be ready.

We must remember that these people carried in their heritage knowledge of civilizations and catastrophes that we can only guess at. If we believe the stories of floods that destroyed cultures we can't even begin to imagine, we can realize that these people were not naked savages but rather the remnants of great empires. They retained some of their knowledge, using it in religious and mundane ways. Certain talents and abilities would not have been eliminated by the successive thundering waters. Memories cannot be washed away, nor can abilities.

Water, when it is rising and destroying, can be a frightening thing. Ask anyone who has been caught in a tidal wave or has had home and property destroyed by a raging river. Then imagine this "wave" and this "river" engulfing vast cities, highways, institutes of science and learning. Imagine the people afterward. Imagine the *United States* as we know it today washed from shore to shore by waters that swept everything in their path, waters that stayed for months until they formed new rivers and outlets to the oceans. What would remain after such a catastrophe? Who would hold the leadership of such a country? Who would be the intellectuals and the scientists after such a deluge? What would happen to the knowledge that had been placed in books and on computer tapes? Who would be left to interpret it and who would be saved in the struggle to merely survive and start rebuilding?

And suppose that enough people did survive and that enough knowledge survived to pass from father to son and suppose the rebuilding began and then suppose—fifty-two years later—the United States was suddenly devastated again. More deaths, more destruction, more knowledge forever lost. What kind of culture would we have? And how much *permanent* rebuilding would we do if we feared another flood at any moment?

This may have actually happened to the peoples of the earth. Not once, but four times over a span of a mere 829 years! It's a wonder man himself survived, not to mention learning and religion. The ancients of Mexico remembered their "myths" about a great flood so clearly that they charted the planet Venus and watched her movements closely. No wonder they venerated Quetzalcoatl when he "burned himself up" and took control of this destructive star. He literally sacrificed himself to save them.

"For God gave his only begotten son . . ."

# 4.

# Moctezuma and Cortez

Because Quetzalcoatl said he would return in 1519, that year the Aztec leader Moctezuma had couriers everywhere. They fanned out across his empire looking for the first signs of the god's return.

In truth, Moctezuma wasn't that eager to see Quetzalcoatl. He had ascended to the throne in 1502 as the ninth hereditary ruler of the Aztec people, both a man and a god in his own right. Revered by his subjects, he exacted his tribute of gold and lives, and surrounded himself with beautiful women, most of them daughters of other warlords. He was slender, well built, and not as dark-skinned as many of his subjects. He bathed three times a day and never wore the same clothes twice. Once he had discarded them, they were burned.

The Spanish historian Bernal Diaz, who met Moctezuma

and had many chances to observe him, wrote: "His cooks prepared over thirty kinds of dishes for every meal and they placed small pottery braziers under them so they wouldn't get cold. They cooked chicken, turkey, pheasant, partridge, quail, tame and wild duck, venison, wild pig, hares and rabbits. The ruler sat at a low stool that was soft and richly ornamented. The table was also low and spread with white cloths and napkins. Four beautiful and clean women brought water so he could wash his hands after every course.

"From time to time they would serve him from cups of pure gold a certain drink made from cacao. For entertainment, ugly humpback dwarfs would dance and sing. After he finished his meal and after the jesters and singers had retired, he would take a decorated tube mixed with liquid amber and an herb they call tabaco [sic] and he would smoke one of these tubes and with it fall asleep."

Moctezuma had been reared for the good life. In his youth he had gone through the college for warriors, then the college for priests. As leader he had to experience both sides of these two most important aspects of his nation's culture. For he would become not only the head of the government, but commander-in-chief of the army and high priest of the temples as well. In the religious college he had heard of the Toltecs and had studied the life of Quetzalcoatl; and it bothered him that this great god would return while he, Moctezuma, was still on the throne. He considered it a cruel injustice that after all his work, he would be removed by someone over whom he had no authority and with no chance of compromising.

He had worked while he was ruler. He led his armies into battle and conquered some 375 towns under the Aztec banner. He resolved civil cases with the justice of Solomon and when he thought one of his ministers wasn't behaving correctly, he would disguise himself as a common man and observe the minister incognito.

He respected Quetzalcoatl's power, but was fearful of the reprisals the god would hand down when he saw how his teachings had been twisted to satisfy the Aztec leaders and priests who had come after him. Rulers before Moctezuma had insisted that prisoners be sacrificed to the God of the Sun, and many concentration camps had been set up outside Mexico City holding thousands of warriors and political enemies to be killed in honor of the powerful but dreaded sun god. Quetzalcoatl was against human sacrifice. He had said as much. He was against one man killing another even in battle. What would he think when he came back to see the daily ritual slaughter being done in his name? When a new temple had been inaugurated in the plaza at Tenochtitlán, twenty-five thousand prisoners from every province under his rule had been sacrificed to the god. For three solid weeks, priests ripped open bodies and thrust their hands in to tear out the hearts. Then they would hold them toward the sun, thus giving it new energy and new blood to continue to shine. When the priests became weary, the common people were ordered to help them in their massacre. Moctezuma remembered the stench, the rivers of blood, the hundreds of carts that carried away the bodies. He knew Quetzalcoatl would hold him personally responsible.

One day a messenger came running into the royal palace. Strange men with hair on their faces and with white skins had been seen on the east coast. Soon other messengers arrived with paintings on rough cloth that showed many white men dressed in iron. They came from eleven enormous canoes that seemed to be powered by the wind god held prisoner in snares of huge cloth. These white strangers rode atop large deer that snorted and ran but had no antlers. They also had enormous dogs whose tongues hung out and whose teeth were sharp.

Moctezuma's aides suggested he flee to another city, arm the warriors, and march against these few odd strangers. After all, said his generals, they had conquered larger groups than these. But for the first time in his life Moctezuma was afraid. These strangers were obviously gods, obviously led by Quetzalcoatl. His end was near. His reign was over. He was not quite forty years old. The Aztec people were doomed. Their religion and their armies would be destroyed. It had been decreed thousands of years before his time. It had been decreed, but it just wasn't fair.

He decided to take no action. What could he do? So he waited in his palace for the gods to approach. And by waiting he allowed a few mercenary adventurers to change the entire course of Latin America.

Cortez was hardly a god. Just thirty-four years old, he had lived more than a man twice his age. He still carried a scar on his chest from a rooftop fall when he had been forced to flee to avoid an angry husband who came home unexpectedly. His parents despaired of ever making anything of him. Much against their meager income they sent him to the University in Salamanca, but he stayed for only two years. It is still a historical question as to whether he left voluntarily or was asked to leave. When he was nineteen he managed to sail to the New World and landed at Santo Domingo, Spain's capital of Española. By using his cleverness he soon had a large grant of land and several hundred Indian slaves. The slaves sold for four pesos each and those who refused to work were burned at the stake before the others. When one managed to escape, he was hunted down with specially trained dogs and his bloody carcass brought back to rot in the sun as a lesson to other slaves.

Cortez liked running a farm. It suited his personality, but soon he tired of it and turned his land and slaves into gold. He had heard of an Indian city in what is today known as the Yucatan. The governor of Cuba, Diego Velasquez, had also heard of this city and gave Cortez a commission to go there and establish trade routes between these people and Cuba. Instead, Cortez armed the eleven trading ships with guns and a motley crew of five hundred adventurers and ex-convicts. When the governor heard of the plans he ordered Cortez to stop, but the ships had already sailed.

Cortez arrived at the Yucatan village and immediately

slew as many Indians as he could, burned the houses, and took a beautiful girl prisoner. He baptized her with the name Doña Marina. At first he gave her to one of his men, then took her back for himself. Later she bore him a son and learned Spanish, thereby becoming one of the most valuable assets in his conquest by acting as interpreter. Not only could she speak the Mayan tongue, but the Nahuatl language of the Aztecs as well. It was Doña Marina who told him of the legendary city in the central plateau. She had never been there, but traders had told her of the enormous stone pyramids, the lavish crops, the luxurious life of the rulers, and the gold and silver that seemed to grow on trees. Cortez wanted that gold and he set his sails toward Veracruz. Doña Marina guided him every step of the way.

Today this woman is still hated by her own people. They say they can hear her voice along the rivers and sweeping through the mountains. It is always mourning, always crying, always seeking forgiveness for the destruction she helped bring about. But the Mexicans have no intention of forgiving her.

After landing at Veracruz, Cortez made his way overland toward Mexico City. He passed through several small towns and was delighted to learn that these people were tired of the Aztec yoke and were more than happy to join him in Moctezuma's overthrow. At each village he gained more soldiers. At each village he was offered gold and precious jewels. His armies increased as rapidly as his avarice.

At one of his stops, messengers from the Aztec chieftain arrived bearing gifts and offers of peace. Moctezuma wanted to pave the way with friendship. He wanted Quetzalcoatl to like him when he finally arrived in his capital. Therefore, to save his own skin and reputation, nothing was too fine for these approaching gods.

Bernal Diaz wrote of these first amazing presents: "A disk of the finest gold and as large as a cartwheel! It was a wonderful thing to see. There were twenty ducks made of gold and other beautifully wrought pieces in the forms of dogs, tigers, lions, and monkeys." There were ten neck-laces of incredibly beautiful workmanship and a dozen arrows made of gold. Two bows to shoot them with were also of gold. Even the drawstring was a cord of pure gold.

To please Quetzalcoatl, Moctezuma sent him his ser-pent mask carved from a single piece of turquoise adorned with rare quetzal feathers. A necklace of precious green stones outlined in gold was also included. For his feet, sandals of the finest obsidian.

Cortez thanked the messengers and gave each of them a handful of glass beads in return. He also gave them a rusted helmet and told them when he arrived in their capital city he expected it to be filled with gold nuggets. He also demanded a golden throne to sit on when he met Moctezuma face to face.

"By this gold," wrote Bernal Diaz, "we knew they had good mines, knowledge worth more to us than all the gifts they had presented." Cortez also knew there was more where these came from, and so he sent all these treasures to Spain as gifts to his king, Carlos V. It was a diplomatic ploy, for he knew that the governor of Cuba must have reported his illegal armada to Spain and that the king probably wanted his scalp. He knew that the king was as gold-hungry as himself, and that these "small advance gifts of respect" would guarantee his legal safety in this new land and assure his appointment as governor of all he could conquer in the name of Spain. (Carlos V put the art objects on display for several weeks, then had them melted down into ingots. So much for royal aesthetics.)

His march toward Mexico City was covered in blood and gold. When he arrived in Tlaxcala he had his original Spanish soldiers and two thousand Totonac warriors with him. The Tlaxcalans, also anxious to overthrow the Aztec rulers, gave him five thousand more warriors.

When he came to Cholula, where the large pyramid dedicated to Quetzalcoatl stands, he camped on the outskirts of the city and received the rulers and priests. They said he could come in, and indeed they wanted to hear what he had to say, but they didn't want their Tlaxcalan enemies inside the sacred area. Cortez promised. The delighted townspeople welcomed him and his Spanish men into their homes and temples. For three days they fed them, danced for them, and gave them gifts. On the third day the entire population gathered in the courtyard of the great pyramid to hear "Quetzalcoatl" speak. As he mounted the altar, his men closed off the entrances. They opened fire with their muskets and advanced with swords and spears. The Tlaxcalan warriors helped slaughter everyone in sight. The entire population, some five thousand persons unsuspecting and unarmed, lay dead in less than an hour. Onward he marched, his army of vindictive Tlaxcalans glad for any encounter with their life-long foes.

Cortez kept up a one-sided correspondence with Carlos V, telling him of his conquests in the name of Spain. In one letter he mentioned coming upon a large town: "Since I surprised them, they were unarmed. The women and children ran naked in the streets, and I fell upon them and permitted none to escape."

As they continued their march, the soldiers dressed their wounds with the fat of Indians they killed along the way. Then, on November 8, he reached the waterway that surrounded the Aztec capital. On orders from their leader, the people were out in droves. They knelt and pressed their hands to the ground as a sign of holy submission to this god. From a litter of gold, studded with precious stones and decorated with multi-colored feathers, Moctezuma came forward to meet Cortez.

"Are you," Cortez asked suspiciously, "are you Moctezuma?"

"I am he," replied the doomed ruler, and he placed around Cortez' neck a necklace of gold and silver that hung down to his waist. Then, reports Fray Bernardino de Sahagún, Moctezuma said, "Oh, our lord, you have arrived on Earth; you have come to your noble city of Mexico. I have been troubled for a long time. I have gazed into the unknown from where you have come. That place of mystery, the land of the sky and stars. The rulers of old are gone, but they said you would return. Now it is ful-filled. You have returned. Welcome now to your land. Visit your palace that you may rest your body."

After that it was like "A Thousand and One Nights" for the Spanish soldiers. They saw the carved temples, the immaculate whitewashed city and a bustling marketplace bigger than anything in Europe. They saw the inner rooms of the sacrificial temples with human hearts burning before magnificent stone idols, and priests, their golden robes so encrusted with blood that "even in the slaughterhouses of Castile there was no such stink." They watched religious ceremonies and a game played with golden balls. But Cortez had not come for religion or sports. He had come for gold and he demanded it. A conversation between Moctezuma and Cortez was reported like this:

"Why do you have to have so much gold?"

"We are troubled with a disease of the heart," replied Cortez, "for which gold is the only remedy."

Moctezuma took him to a room in the palace filled with gold nuggets, slabs of silver, and baskets of gems. There were ropes of pearls, hundreds of pieces of jewelry, cloth embroidered with gold and silver fibers and table settings of solid gold. Cortez had his men haul it all away and melt it down into ingots. A Royal Fifth was set aside for Carlos V. Cortez took another fifth, and what was left was divided among his Spanish soldiers. Then, still not happy with more wealth than he had ever possessed before, he demanded that Moctezuma show him the loca-tions of the gold mines.

While Moctezuma was making up his mind about this request (for he had begun to have doubts about these "gods") a message came for Cortez. Back in Veracruz where he had left some of his men to guard the ships, two of his Spanish soldiers had been killed by Totonac Indians. Cortez demanded that the leader of the Totonacs come to Mexico City at once to explain this deed.

The man arrived with his young son and fourteen dignitaries. He explained to Cortez what the Spaniards had done and why they had been put to death. Then Cortez had them shackled and he led them personally into the courtyard of Moctezuma's palace. He burned them alive.

Seeing this, Moctezuma knew that the great Quetzalcoatl would never do such a barbaric thing. Obviously these white-skinned strangers were not gods, but some sort of demons, enemies of everything Quetzalcoatl stood for. Moctezuma told Cortez he would never reveal the site of the gold mines.

Immediately Cortez had Moctezuma placed in chains. The Aztecs heard of it and became restless. They began to talk of mutiny and death to the white men, but still they were confused. Moctezuma and the priests had said this man was Quetzalcoatl. He didn't act like Quetzalcoatl, and his men certainly didn't act like lesser gods. And they had put their priest-leader-deity into prison.

Cortez saw what was brewing for him, and so with seventy trusted men and as much gold as he could cart away, he hurried back to Veracruz and his waiting ships. He had no intention of dying in an Aztec temple. When he arrived he found nineteen ships with about one thousand men whom the governor of Cuba had sent to capture him and bring him back to justice. There was a quick battle. The Tlaxcalan warriors overtook the lead ship and killed the Spanish captains. Once he showed the new sailors all that gold, it didn't take Cortez long to win them over to his side. Now armed with thirteen hundred Spanish soldiers and two thousand Tlaxcalan warriors, Cortez headed back toward Mexico City and the final conquest of Moctezuma.

While he was on his way, the men he had left back in Mexico City had taken matters into their own hands. The yearly celebration to Huitzilopochtli, the god of all gods, had taken place. This year it had been especially splendid because the priests wanted the white men to see their devotion; if Cortez was Quetzalcoatl, his men would tell him how worthy they really were.

Only the bravest warriors, who had proven their valor in battle, were allowed to participate in these ceremonies. Young men, the pride of the military college, also took part, along with other youths who had fasted and prayed. The Dance of the Serpent was the high point of the ceremonies. When it began, the Spanish soldiers attacked.

The drummer was the first to go. His arms were chopped off and then his head. Then death came to the cream of Aztec youth. An onlooker reported: "These fell instantly to the ground with their entrails hanging out. Others were beheaded. Some were struck in the shoulders where their arms were torn from their bodies. Others were struck in their abdomens and their entrails spilled onto the ground. Some tried to escape, their entrails dragging as they ran, but the Spaniards murdered them at the gates. Others climbed the walls, but they could not save themselves. The blood of the warriors flowed like water and gathered into pools." Then the victorious white men, having caught everyone by surprise, invaded the nearby houses, killing and burning everyone they encountered. The Aztec people now knew these men were not gods and rose up against them, backing them into the area around Moctezuma's palace.

Cortez and his army arrived just at this time and also ran for cover to the palace. He had not expected this welcome and was unprepared for it. The newcomers with him didn't want to fight. They wanted gold and told him so.

Moctezuma was removed from his chains and Cortez told him to give his people orders to stop the fighting. If his men could leave the city, he promised he would not come back again.

Moctezuma didn't believe him. Why should he? But he was a prisoner and resigned to his fate. After this latest bloodbath, he knew his own people would never respect him again. Now his people knew that, at the heart of the matter, it was Moctezuma's fault that things had turned out as they did.

He came out on a rooftop of the palace. Once the crowds were silenced he began to speak of peace and love. He begged his people to stop their fighting and permit the white men to leave the city. The answer was a hail of stones. They struck Moctezuma and knocked him down.

Historians still are not certain if he was killed by these stones or by the Spanish. Maybe it was the psychological weight of everything that had happened. But Moctezuma was dead. Someone tossed his body to the crowd below and it was put upon a pyre where "it lay sizzling and smelled foul as it burned."

The fighting raged for four more days, then a calm set in. For seven more days Cortez and his men studied the situation. Then finally one rainy night—*La Noche Triste*: The Sad Night—they tried to escape the city. But a woman saw them and screamed the news. Through the rain came Aztec warriors, slaughtering everyone they could reach. Over half the Spaniards perished, most of them unable to fight back because of the huge amounts of gold they carried. Thousands of Tlaxcalan warriors also died. Cortez managed to escape, but not before he was badly wounded in the head and had lost two fingers.

The Aztecs should have followed them beyond the city gates, but, leaderless and disorganized, they permitted the few survivors to escape. The Otomi people gave them food and lodging.

Cortez waited a full year. Then with his forces, augmented by over two hundred thousand Indian warriors, he returned to Mexico City. Quite by accident, his troops also returned with the deadliest weapon of all: smallpox.

For eighty days the beleaguered Aztecs fought off the invaders. There was little food inside the city and many died of starvation. There was no fresh water. Some even ate dirt to stay alive. Weakened and with no real leader, it is said, over two hundred forty thousand Aztecs died from smallpox. (More than thirty thousand of Cortez' warriors died from it as well.) When the fighting stopped and the Spaniards entered the city, it was a wasteland of rotting bodies and sickening stench. Almost all the nobles were dead, as were all the soldiers and most of the old people. Only a few little children and some women remained. The disaster Moctezuma had feared had come true.

From the destroyed city, Cortez sent his trusted captains to subdue the rest of the country. One by one, the great peoples fell: Mixtecs, Zapotecs, Tarascans, and the Mayans. Temples were sacked, treasures melted down, and thousands of books destroyed because "they did not carry the name of Jesus Christ inside them."

The Mayans fell easily, by another quirk of fate. Their religious leaders had prophesied that their destruction would come before the period Katun 8 Ahau had ended. When the Spanish appeared only 136 days before the end of that period, the Mayans thought it was the work of the gods and fled quietly into the jungle.

# 5.
# The Virgin of Guadalupe and The Virgin of Las Limas

One of the most beautiful stories they tell in Mexico—a lovely tale full of mystery, apparitions and physical phenomena—is about the apparition of the Virgin of Guadalupe and how she became the patron saint not only of Mexico but of all South America. It goes something like this:

On a Saturday, the 9th of December, 1531, young Juan Diego was hurrying to study his catechism in a church several miles from his home. He was an Indian boy of pure Aztec blood who had recently been converted to Catholicism. So ardent was his conversion that he had tried to convert his uncle Juan Bernardino as well, who had raised him when Juan's mother and father had died. Although a good man, the uncle was none too sure about the religion of the conquerers. It had only been eleven years since the white man had caused such havoc and had destroyed his people's centuries-old culture.

But Juan Diego enjoyed the Church and all it stood for. That's why, on that cold frosty morning, bundled in his long homespun cape, he took a shortcut over the hill of Tepeyac rather than go all the way around it and delay his arrival at the church.

At the top of the hill he stopped short. Someone was calling his name. As he listened, there was the most beautiful music and the sound of hundreds of song-birds. He followed the sounds until he came to the very peak of the hill. There, to his great astonishment, stood a beautiful Indian girl. She was about nineteen years of age, but dressed in flowing robes like saints in the paintings he had seen at church. She was barefoot and stood on a rock, but the rock sparkled as if made of precious stones. "Juan Diego," she said softly, and he came closer. Her skin was as dark as his, and her hands were clasped together as if in prayer.

"Where are you going, my son?" she asked in his native Nahuatl. When he replied that he was going to the church at Tlateloco to study the life of the Saviour Jesus Christ, she smiled.

The story goes that this lovely teenage Indian girl then said the following flowery phrases to the little Indian boy. By an even bigger miracle, he later remembered enough to recount them word for word.

"Understand and pay attention," she said, "you who are the smallest of my sons, that I am the Sacred Virgin Mary, mother of the true God for which we live, the Creator of the world, the Maker of heaven and earth. I fervently desire that a temple should be erected here on this spot. It should be a testament of my love, my compassion, my help, and my protection, because I am the Blessed Mother of you and of all your people and of all the peoples who love me, confide in me, and seek my help. I will listen to your sorrows and calm your pains and sufferings. Because of all this, I wish you to go to the palace of the Bishop in Mexico City and tell him that I have sent you so that he will manifest my great desire. Explain that here on this hill, a temple should be erected. Tell him word for word of everything you have seen, heard, and wondered at. And go with confidence that I will be pleased and that I will reward you. I will make your life happy and will make you worthy of the tasks that you undertake in my name. Now you, the smallest of my sons, have heard my wishes; so go and do your duty."

Little Juan Diego was filled with love for this beautiful lady and promised to go immediately and tell the Bishop. He walked down the hill toward the palace which was almost four miles away. But when he arrived, the guards refused to let him in. He pleaded with them and told them his story. Finally, he was admitted into the Bishop's study. He immediately fell on his knees before this awesome representative of Holy Rome and told his story exactly as it had happened.

The Bishop, Fray Juan de Zumarraga, was not impressed. As the first Catholic Bishop to the newly conquered country of Mexico, he had heard a lot of stories from pious, converted Indians. This tale might even have been the work of the Devil. Obviously the youth had made it all up. "It's all quite interesting," he told the boy, "but I need some time to think about it. I'll let you know of my decision." And with that the boy was led back onto the street.

Juan Diego returned to the hill, sad and worried over what the Virgin would say about his failure. She was waiting for him in all her raiment, her lights, and her music. He fell to his knees and told her everything that the Bishop had said. Then he added, "My lady, send someone else in my place the next time, someone of importance. I am nobody. The Bishop will not listen to me."

"Listen to *me,* my smallest of sons," she said, "you must understand that I have many messengers and servants who could carry my wishes and make them known. But it is absolutely necessary that you be the one to carry out this task. I urgently ask you and definitely order you to go back again tomorrow and see the Bishop again. Give him orders in my name and make him understand that he must construct the temple that I wish."

You would think it would have been easier for her to have appeared in front of the Bishop herself and saved all that traveling, but back again the next day went little Juan Diego. Again it wasn't easy to see the great man, but the guards finally permitted him an audience. The Bishop listened a little more closely to his story this time and asked him many questions about the apparition. He repeated word for word everything that the lady had said and ended up ordering the Bishop in the Virgin's name to build her a temple atop the hill of Tepeyac.

The Bishop told him that while he *almost* believed the story, he couldn't just start building churches on every hill around Mexico City. He said he needed more proof, something solid upon which to base his decision. "If this lady really is the Holy Mother," he said, "tell her to give me a sign." Juan promised to deliver this message to the lady, and left the room.

Then the Bishop called two of his trusted aides and told them to follow the boy and report everything they saw. Keeping a discreet distance behind Juan Diego, they watched him leave the city, watched him climb the hill of Tepeyac and then—much to their chagrin—they watched him vanish. Furious and feeling foolish that they had let a mere Indian boy outwit them, they returned to the palace and told the Bishop the child was a liar and that he shouldn't listen to anything else he had to say.

Meanwhile, Juan Diego had reached the top of the hill. The lady appeared and he told her that the Bishop wanted a sign. "Come by here tomorrow," she said, "and I shall give you a sign to take to the Bishop, and it shall be one that he cannot deny." Then she vanished.

Juan went to his home, but when he arrived he discovered that his uncle was in agony. He had contracted a deadly disease and was slowly dying. Juan nursed him all through the night and all through the next day. He did not keep his appointment with the vision.

On Monday, the 11th of December, Juan convinced his dying uncle to see a priest. He wanted him to make his confession and receive the blessing of the holy oils. The boy headed out toward the church of Tlateloco when he remembered that the lady had been kept waiting. Ashamed of his actions, he decided to take the long road around the hill rather than go up over the top. That way he wouldn't have to face her and explain why he hadn't kept his appointment.

But the lady was waiting for him on the lower path. "What happened to you, my smallest son?" she asked. "Why are you on this path and not the one at the top of the hill?"

In a torrent of words he told the story of his uncle and how sorry he was that the man was dying and also how unworthy he was of carrying out any further work for this lovely lady.

"Listen," she said, "your uncle is well. I have been to see him right after you left the house, and he is cured. Trust in me. There is no reason to worry about him any longer. You must now carry out my orders. Go to the top of the hill and you will see many flowers growing. Pick a large bundle of them and wrap them in your cape. Then take them to the Bishop. They will be the sign that he is seeking. Take care and show the flowers to no one but the Bishop. Do not let anyone else touch them." And she vanished.

Juan climbed to the top of the hill and there saw hundreds of red roses. It surprised him because it was cold and frosty, and not at all the season for roses. He smelled them and was delighted with their fragrance. As he picked several dozen, he noted that they were still covered with dew. He pressed them against his stomach and brought the end of his cape up and over them. Thus hidden from view, he carried the roses to the door of the Bishop's palace.

The guards knew him by this time and refused to let

him enter. They had been given orders by the Bishop himself that this little liar wasn't to come in. Then they demanded to know what it was he carried in his cape. They could smell the perfume. They grabbed the cape and forced it open. They saw the roses and reached for them. But a strange thing happened. The live roses turned into painted roses—flowers painted on the inside of his cape. Now the guards had something to report to the Bishop and they ran telling him of the incident. Of course, Juan Diego was ushered into the throne room immediately.

This time the boy did not kneel. "You asked for a sign," he said, "and the lady told me to give you these roses. She said you would understand what they meant." He let down the front of his cape, and fresh roses spilled onto the floor at the Bishop's feet. While others in the room gasped at seeing the flowers, the Bishop was staring at the cape. For there, painted on this rough-woven Indian blanket, was an image of Our Lady.

Then Juan Diego looked and sure enough, it was a painting of the young girl who had appeared four times to him on the hill. "This is the lady who sent me," he said simply.

The Bishop had Juan take off the cape and stared at the painted image. It showed a young Indian girl, her eyes closed and her face inclined in prayer. Her black hair hung to her shoulders. Her hands were together in an upright position against her breast, fingertips touching. She wore a red robe decorated in gold, with lace at the collar and cuffs. Over this she wore a blue cape bordered in gold and decorated with small gold stars. Her one visible foot was wearing a golden slipper and she was standing on a golden crescent moon. Under the moon and holding her robe and mantle was a white-faced, brown-haired angel with blue wings tipped in red. He wore a red robe, but the circle of clouds around him and the Virgin obscured him from the waist down. All around the figure of the girl was an aura of dazzling sunburst yellow.

The Bishop took this painting into his private chapel

where he prayed and thanked God and the Blessed Mother for the miracle. Then he let Juan Diego lead him to the spot where the lady wished her temple to be built. Juan and his uncle lived the rest of their days in the Bishop's palace and never wanted for a thing.

Today this image is known all over Spanish-speaking America. The humble cape has become the most important religious relic in the New World. The lady got her temple. It stands in the center of an emormous plaza, made of red brick and white cement and embellished with towers, sculptures, and crosses. Every day of the year you can see Mexicans coming to honor their Lady of Guadalupe. Those who have made promises to her fall on their knees and hobble across the rough stones of the plaza more than a city block away from the door to the cathedral. On their knees they go up the steps then down the aisle, all the way down to the altar railing where they can look up and see, hanging quite high and in shadows, the miraculous cape of little Juan Diego.

When you take the tour the guide will tell you that the painting is still as fresh today as it was when it first appeared almost four hundred and fifty years ago. He will tell you that there are no brush strokes to be seen any-where on it, that the colors have been examined under the best microscopes in the world and are not ordinary paints at all. He will tell you that experts have examined the image and have all declared that they have no idea how it was painted. "The hand of man," my guide told me, "is nowhere to be seen." So you stand looking up at this psychic treasure wishing you could get closer, wishing the lighting was better, wishing you didn't have to take the guide's word for everything.

Well, you don't.

In 1974, Manuel Toledano Hernandez wrote a book called *The Apparitions at Tepeyac: Myth or Reality?* In it, the Mexican historian and reporter discloses a few things that throw a different light on both legend and painting.

First of all, the legend had never been heard of until

the year 1648, when a booklet was published in Mexico City called "The Image of the Virgin Mary." It was written by a Manuel Sánchez, who told the story—for the first time—of Juan Diego and the miraculous painting. This was 127 years *after* the miracle had supposedly taken place. Sánchez said he got it from a booklet he found published in the Nahuatl language and in his preface said he would reprint the booklet at the end of his book. There was no reprint included.

Secondly, in all the voluminous letters, documents, and diaries extant of Bishop Fray Juan de Zumarraga, there is not one word regarding the miracle. The Bishop went back to Spain in 1532 for a year's stay and speech-making about his new territory, and not once did he mention the appearance of Our Lady on the Indian cloak. Bishop de Zumarraga was a vain man who was constantly looking out for his own interests. Most certainly if he had been the witness and the main contact between Juan Diego and the Mother of God, he would have let everyone know it. But he never uttered a word.

One of Spain's most excellent historians of the Mexican people, Fray Bernardino de Sahagún, arrived two years before the supposed vision and spent the rest of his life interviewing Indians and writing of their religious beliefs. It seems most likely he would have mentioned the vision, and, with his reporter's zeal, have interviewed Juan Diego personally. But again, not a word is found in his writings.

Other priests came to Mexico and returned to Spain with written reports of what they had seen. None mentioned the Virgin of Guadalupe.

In 1556, the head of the Franciscan Order in Mexico, Fray Francisco de Bustamante, preached a sermon at the tiny church atop Tepeyac hill and then blasted the Indians for their belief in "an idolatrous image painted by an Indian named Marcos." He told the churchmen there—and later repeated it at a special hearing—that Rome did not want the Indians to have their pagan idols taken from them only to be replaced by Christian idols. "They must learn that God is everywhere and not in some inferior painting." Instead of being sent back to Spain immediately (or tried for heresy) Fray Bustamante lived a long and full life in Mexico City.

In the 1930s, one of Mexico's top artists, Jorge González Camarena, was given the job of restoring the murals at the Huejotingo Convent in the city of Puebla, the first convent built by the Spanish in Mexico. Imagine his surprise when he uncovered, under layers of chalky repainting, an image of the Virgin Mary almost identical in every way to the Lady of Guadalupe.

"It was the work of a great indigenous artist," he told a magazine reporter in 1971, "and is indeed a masterpiece equal to anything that Rafael or Murillo had done in Europe. Because of my position I was fortunate enough to be allowed to examine the painting that hangs in the Basilica of Guadalupe. After comparing the lines, the use of colors and, most importantly, the brush strokes, I can definitely state that both works were done by the same artist."

Bernal Diaz del Castillo, writer, Spanish soldier, and cohort of Cortez, wrote the now classic *The True History of the Conquest of New Spain.* In Chapter XCI he states that there existed then in Mexico a school of native painters who had been trained by a Franciscan father to "copy images and make perfect reliquaries that without a doubt compare with the best work being done in Italy and Spain." Bernal Diaz then lists the three top painters of this school: Juan de la Cruz, "El Crespillo," and Marcos de Aquino.

So why all the mystery? Why the subterfuge? Why the need to invent the story of the Virgin of Guadalupe?

When the Spanish arrived, the Aztecs had a temple of their own atop Tepeyac hill. It was a temple to Tenotzin, the *virgin* mother of all the Aztec gods and mother of all the Mexicans. Each year, on December 22 of the European calendar, the Indians would come from miles around for ceremonies and special services to this goddess. At the time of Bishop Zumarraga these festivities and adorations were still going on and they continued for more than a hundred years until the Church *invented* the story of an apparition of an Indian *virgin* who claimed to be the protector of all the Indians and demanded a temple erected in her honor at the same site where the homage to Tenotzin took place.

A history was written, an image of Our Lady was found. A papal decree said she was to be honored on the 12th and not the 22nd day of December, and Indian superstition took over from there. Throughout medieval Europe, pagan temples had been refurbished as Christian basilicas. Once again, the Catholic Church triumphed in their motto of "If you can't lick 'em, join 'em."

Hernandez' exposé rocked Mexico for a short time, but did nothing to convince the Mexicans that their Lady wasn't for real. They had seen too many miracles, witnessed too many healings, had heard too many stories to believe anything that Hernandez—or any other reporter—could come up with. They still crawl on their knees toward the shadowy painting. They still offer it gold and silver charms, bouquets of flowers, and name their daughters Guadalupe. Who cares about facts? They *know* the Virgin of Guadalupe is for real. They know she is *their* Divine Lady, their personal direct Mexican link with God.

Venerations come quickly to the Mexican people, especially those in isolated rural areas who have grown up listening to stories about Catholic saints and Aztec gods.

On July 16, 1965, the Day of the Virgin of Carmen, two children, Severiano and Rosita Salazar, went into the jungle near their Las Limas home in tropical Veracruz State. They had some nuts they wanted to eat and needed a flat stone to crack the shells. They saw a greenish rock in the ground. As they smoothed away the earth, their curiosity grew, for the more earth they cleared from the stone, the bigger it got. Finally they dug down around it and to their horror discovered a face. Thinking it was a human face that had turned to stone, they ran for their father who was working in a nearby field.

He began to dig and uncovered a large image 22 inches high and weighing 132 pounds. The image, in highly polished jade-like stone, was of a seated figure holding a child in its arms.

Immediately the farmer thought it was a statue of Our Lady, and who else could she be holding but the Christ Child? He and the children managed to get it back to their straw and palm-leaf house where he set the image on a makeshift altar wrapped in a white sheet.

The news spread all through the sparsely populated area. An image had been found of Our Lady! And by two small children, exactly on the day of Our Lady of Carmen! It was a miracle, a message, a blessing for the poor people of the area!

By the dozens countrymen began to come to see the image and cover it with flowers, light candles, and burn sweet-smelling roots and bark. Miracles began to occur. A man bitten by a snake survived when his wife lit a candle to this Virgin of Las Limas. An old woman was able to throw away her cane after she kissed the image of the Virgin of Las Limas. It was truly a blessed day when the Salazar children went looking for a stone!

A Mexican ethnologist heard about the Virgin and, accompanied by three other professional people, went to see it. They had to travel by ·canoe to reach the small village. Even though the cult had been going on for only nine days, when they were shown the image they could hardly see the carving for the flowers and the offerings piled around it.

The ethnologist studied the carving and then gave the villagers the news—good for him, sad for them. It was not an image of the Virgin, but a statue of an Olmec priest. That was not the Child Jesus on its lap, but rather a baby jaguar, an animal revered by the Olmecs. The expert told the disappointed villagers that he would have to take the statue to the museum in Jalapa, since such pre-colonial works of art belonged exclusively to the Mexican government. The farmers agreed to let the idol, go, providing that the government would give them in exchange a school for their children and settle a public land-distribution argument. The terms were agreeable to the experts, and the statue was removed to Jalapa.

There it sat for five years, surrounded by other pieces of Olmec art, until one night someone forced the lock on the door and broke a window of the museum. The watchmen found blood all over the floor leading in a trail out to where a car had been parked. From the badly forced door and the bloodstained window, the robbery was obviously the work of amateurs. Of all the other potentially marketable pre-colonial works in the museum, the Virgin of Las Limas was the only one missing.

But the priceless statue never came up for sale at any of the known clandestine art outlets. The authorities checked everywhere, interviewed dozens of dealers and collectors. The statue was nowhere to be found.

But the village of Las Limas never got its school and never had its land problem solved. Rumor has it that the statue is back in the village, hidden from all outsiders. They never believed it was an Olmec priest anyway. Somewhere, the Virgin of Las Limas continues to work her miracles.

# 6.
# Mystical Christian Healers: Teresa Urrea, Fidencio, and Monica Lopez

Mexico's psychic history is filled with "miracle healings." One of the most famous was the lady known as "The Saint of Cabora." She was born Teresa Urrea in the mountains of northern Sinaloa State in 1873. Her family was very poor, and Teresa was a frail child. She could be seen bringing food to the ill around the town and caring for stray dogs and cats. One day she had an epileptic attack and fell unconscious to the ground. She was taken home. Her anxious family and neighbors watched her breathing get weaker and weaker. Finally there was no breath at all. A coffin was made, flowers were picked, and Teresa's body was prepared for burial. But she awoke and smiled. The myth began: she had risen from the dead, they said. She is a saint.

After this experience, Teresa began to heal. When she

touched them, the crippled threw away their crutches. The blind saw. Diseases were halted. A wealthy rancher opened his farm to her, and she began to work on hundreds of the faithful who climbed the mountain every day to see her. The ranch was named Cabora and her sanctuary became the most venerated spot in northern Mexico. Those around her did a brisk business in the sale of bottles of blessed water, amulets, talismans, special incense, and pictures of Teresa.

In 1891 armed rebels in the Sierra Madre mountains broke out in revolt against the central government in Mexico City. Their flag carried a design of Teresa with a golden halo, and their battle cry was *"Viva la santa de Cabora!"* When federal troops attacked, Teresa and her father fled to safety across the border to Nogales, Arizona, where she set up another healing center. But she was unable to stay out of politics. Whether she brought it on herself by her impassioned sermons or because she just happened to be a mystical rallying point is not clear, but in 1896 a small army of Yaqui and Mayo Indians attacked the customs office at Nogales, shouting *"Viva la santa de Cabora!"* The disorders rippled all along the frontier, and the United States authorities told her to stop meddling in politics or she would be arrested. She moved farther north, settling in the small Arizona town of Clifton, where she continued her healings and preachings until she died in 1906 at the age of thirty-three.

The town of Espinazo sits in dusty desert on the borders of Nuevo Leon and Coahuila states. It has about five hundred permanent residents. Once it had over fifty thousand people coming and going daily. But that was back in the days of Niño Fidencio.

The country was ripe for him. In the previous century there had been other "niños" in Mexico: Manuelito, Juanito, Marcelito, Pedrito Jaramillo, and Tatia, but none of them had the impact of Fidencio. He was something special. He was a man of miracles, a healer, a surgeon, a dreamer and one of the most eccentric characters the Mexican psychic world has every produced.

The area was ripe for him. Isolated from large cities, lacking even such basics as running water and electricity, when the people of Espinazo needed medical and spiritual care, they were left to shift for themselves. Doctors never went there; priests visited the shuttered and locked church once or twice a year. The people felt abandoned and were ready to make a hero of anyone who showed an interest in their welfare. Such a hero was Niño Fidencio.

Sometime around 1920, a wounded revolutionary soldier was taken on as a hired hand at a ranch owned by a German emigrant named Von Wernich. The German was impressed that this new man, Enrique Lopez de la Fuente, knew something about Spiritualism. Von Wernich had been fascinated with it in his native country and had been a friend of Mexico's Spiritualist President Francisco Madero. In fact, it was Madero who made it possible for him to buy this ranch near Espinazo. Soon Lopez de la Fuente became manager of the ranch and, somewhere around 1925, decided to hire a cook. He remembered a young man with whom he had gone to grade school who had liked to cook and had also been interested in Spiritualism. He wrote the friend and offered him the job. It was accepted. Fidencio Sintora Constantino arrived in Espinazo as a cook and died there as a legend.

Anyone who watched him for any length of time could see there was something not quite right about Fidencio. He was twenty-seven years old, yet didn't have a hair on his face except for his very light eyebrows which he darkened with a black pencil. His eyes were deep-set and he wore dark glasses to protect them from the sun. His lips were full and thick. He had a ready smile and would grin at the slightest word. His voice was high-pitched, and when he giggled it would be even higher. He had a thick thatch of dark hair—sometimes, because every now and then he would shave his head and rub cooking oil on his bald dome to make it shine. He called Enrique "Papa" and Enrique's children called him "Mama." Malicious rumor had it that his sexual organs were almost nonexistent.

Fidencio was one of twenty-five children born to a poor farmer in the center of the country. His schooling was minimal (as was Enrique Lopez'), and before being offered the cook's position, he worked for several years cutting hemp cactus in the Yucatan. Somewhere along the line Fidencio had become a good cook, a talent most Mexican men refuse to try. He could make as good tortillas as any woman, and his tamales, arroz con pollo, and sugary desserts were the best for miles around.

No one is quite sure how his healing powers were first noticed. Legend has it that, as a boy, he healed his grandmother's broken arm. Legend also has it that his first patient in Espinazo was a dying calf. Fidencio held it in his arms and it jumped onto the ground completely well. It is known that the peons working on the ranch would come to him with their aches and pains and would go away healed. Then he supposedly removed a carbuncle from owner Von Wernich's back. The German, so pleased and so certain of the financial effect this news would have, began a publicity campaign that would have made Madison Avenue proud. "The world must know of these extraordinary powers," he proclaimed as he gave the order for photographers to take pictures of Fidencio and to print them on thousands of posters and leaflets. One of the photos showed Fidencio wearing a white robe tied loosely at the waist with a golden cord. The Sacred Heart of Jesus thumped on his breast as he raised his right hand in blessing and placed his right foot on a half-moon held by a winged cherub.

The impact of these pictures on the illiterate and superstitious peasants in the area was immediate, and they flocked to the ranch to have healings. Some arrived on burros or horses. The rich came in carriages. Some were hauled in hammocks slung on poles. Others were wheeled in homemade carts. As the pilgrims increased, bus companies began to run special lines to Espinazo. The railroad, which gave the area infrequent and bad service, added several cars and scheduled the town for two daily stops.

When the news of this new miracle man arrived in Mexico City, the President of the Republic, Plutarco Elías Calles, accompanied by his Secretary of War and the Governor of Nuevo Leon State, hastened to Espinazo in the presidential train. Fidencio was busy with the sick and dying and refused to go to the station to meet the President. Onlookers tell of how an infuriated Enrique Lopez beat Fidencio in front of them, punishing him for the way he had kept the chief magistrate of Mexico waiting. But onlookers also tell of how Fidencio smiled as he was beaten, it was as if he enjoyed the physical punishment Lopez gave him. "Christ, too, was castigated for his beliefs," he was often heard to say.

In any case, President Calles left the luxury of his private car and went into the squalor that was Fidencio's healing center. He was in there, alone with the healer, for over an hour. When he came out, he was dressed in one of Fidencio's healing robes. He boarded his train and returned to the Capital. No one ever told what ailed the President, but a cure must have taken place, for Calles spoke to everyone of the "miracle" that occurred and every week he sent a boxcar loaded with food, gifts, and money to Fidencio for his clinic.

He also sent a complete surgical kit and upon receiving it, Fidencio began performing operations as well. He would slice out tumors, remove cataracts, tie tendons and—his favorite operation—remove tonsils with these new toys the President had sent. Included in the kit was a surgeon's gown, cap, and face mask which Fidencio adopted as his official uniform.

As time went on, the scalpel got dull, so Fidencio would have one of his assistants (females he called "slaves") break a bottle. After choosing the sharpest piece, he would use it to open a patient's body. When the forceps became rusted and stiff, he tossed them away and used a pair of cheap pliers to remove tonsils and pull out teeth.

The astounding thing is that there was never a case of infection reported from any of these caveman-like operations. Fidencio didn't wear gloves, use anesthetics, or even apply alcohol to an area before he opened it. (Brazilian healer Arigo did the same type of operations in the 1950s and 1960s, claiming that the spirit of a Franciscan monk shone a green antiseptic light on the patient that destroyed all germs. There was never a case of infection with his clients either.)

Fidencio's methods of curing patients who didn't require surgery was just as unorthodox. As the multitudes increased, he didn't have time for the individual laying on of hands, so he had wires and a rope pulley strung from wall to wall in his healing room. He would have several dozen patients lie on the floor. Then, grasping these pulleys to keep his balance, he would walk across their backs, sending the healing energy out of his feet rather than through his hands.

Another favorite method was to have his assistants place crates full of oranges, limes, and lemons on a high platform. Once he had climbed on it, he would let the crowds come in. Then he would toss the fruit into the throng, claiming that whoever was hit was cured.

He would take other crowds of the ill and diseased to a dirty river that ran outside the ranch and make them all wade into it up to their chests. Then he would enter the water himself and, he claimed, the energy from his body would flow into the water and cure everyone around him.

As in any primitive area, the number of mentally unbalanced, congenitally deformed, and mongoloid was appalling. Diet deficiencies, unsanitary birth methods, and syphillis had created an army of monsters that needed medical help but had nowhere to go—except to Fidencio. For them he constructed a special area called the Circle, where they were locked behind high walls with no sanitary conveniences, few beds, and no respite from the blazing sun. His assistants were not permitted to enter the Circle, yet Fidencio walked among the madmen unharmed. Every day he would drag out the bodies of those who had died of natural causes or had been killed during the night. (The death rate at Espinazo was appalling. Statistics show that in 1926 there was not one death in the village, yet between 1927 and 1937, 1,329 persons died. Fidencio never took the blame for these deaths, saying that they would have died whether they stayed at home or had come to him. He never claimed to have absolute powers.)

He loved publicity and kept a photographer near him to record his every move. He liked to dress up in different costumes. One day he would appear like Rudolph Valentino in a riding habit, the next day in a well tailored business suit and tie, and the following day in Christ-like robes. He began to believe his own publicity and would pose draped around a cross or staring at a sculptured image of a crucified Christ whose features bore a remarkable resemblence to his own. At one end of his healing center he had a stage built where his female assistants would put on pantomime plays. He spared no expense on their costumes or scenery. Most of the time they presented allegories representing the sun on the flowers or the moon being hidden by clouds, or something similar where they could dress up in filmy knee-length gowns, wear white silk stockings over their dusky legs, and carry bowers of flowers tied to wire frames. Whenever a Biblical scene was presented, Fidencio always played the role of Christ.

Outside the ranch, on what had been empty desert, a shanty town grew. Enterprising merchants built tar-paper and tin hovels that were rented by the hour. A hundred-room "hotel" was constructed of used boards and tin, the rooms the size of closets with no bathrooms, running water, or electricity. Other merchants built lean-to shops and charged outrageous prices for staples like rice and beans. Fortunes were made overnight by farmers who hauled in loads of fresh fruit and vegetables. Others sold amulets supposedly blessed with the healing powers of the "Saint of Espinazo." Others turned their farm wagons from hauling manure to hauling people. A taxi driver from

Mexico City made so much money in one year that he returned to the Capital and bought a fleet of cars. Three morticians offered twenty-four-hour service, as did five prostitutes. Everyone made money from Fidencio except beer and liquor merchants. He refused to allow alcoholic beverages in Espinazo and once, like Christ in the temple, he destroyed a makeshift bar with his bare hands.

No one knows how much money came to Fidencio during these years. He never charged a cent for his services, but it was understood he would accept gifts. Every day literally truckloads of merchandise, food, poultry, and small animals were taken into the gates of the ranch. Who benefited from it is anybody's guess, because Fidencio never went anywhere or was seen spending money. He stayed on the ranch, healing and receiving the honors of a holy man.

In the mid-1930s, the fickleness of the population began to take its toll on Fidencio. He was arrested twice and twice exonerated for practicing medicine without a license. He began to refuse more people than he saw, and as his health declined he spent more and more time in bed. He also began to drink. People who remember him at that period say he couldn't control his facial muscles or carry on a coherent conversation. He smelled of cheap cane alcohol and would get furious whenever anyone asked him to moderate his drinking. Finally the crowds dwindled to a trickle and Fidencio stayed locked in his room for days at a time, surrounded by empty whiskey bottles. On October 19, 1938 the deranged, lonely "New Messiah," "The Maker of Miracles," "The God Elected" died of cirrhosis of the liver. He had just turned forty.

Immediately a cry of anguish arose all across Mexico. Niño Fidencio was dead! He had given his life for so many, and now was dead at such a tender age! They didn't want to hear that he had drunk himself to death. They wanted to believe the rumors that Enrique Lopez had beaten him to death or that a group of medical doctors had assassinated him in order to get his clientele. They came to the funeral in droves. They sobbed and told reporters of how they had been healed, had been saved, had been given a new chance in life.

People still come to put flowers on his bed and candles on the marble tomb that dominates his healing room. A glass of water sits on the tomb, refilled by a caretaker each time a pilgrim drinks the "holy" water. Twice a year, on March 18 (his saint's day) and October 19 (the anniversary of his death) the faithful and the credulous come back to Espinoza. They parade down the streets wearing red handkerchiefs (his favorite color) and singing hymns of praise to his name. The crippled pray for a miracle as do the cancerous, the tubercular, and the leperous. Walking, falling, stumbling, laughing, chanting, crying, they make their way to the dirty river and plunge in hoping that somehow Niño Fidencio will resurrect long enough to make them well.

If you saw the girl with her short dark hair and the large wooden cross hanging around her neck in a crowd of teenagers, you wouldn't give her any special notice. She is pretty in a healthy sort of way, and her features are those of a million other Mexican girls. Yet it is not Monica's physical characteristics that make her unique, but her deep spiritual conviction that Jesus the Christ works his healing power through her.

Monica Lopez has been a mystical phenomenon in Mexico since she was a few months old, when her entire family heard loud noises coming from her bedroom. Looking in, they saw her toys and teddy bear flying through the air and bouncing off the walls. Monica remained asleep and blissfully unaware of what was going on. It was a "miracle," onlookers said.

It was a "miracle" that Monica is even alive. When she was born, on May 4, 1958, the doctors told her parents the child needed an operation immediately. Her intestines were blocked, and without surgery there was no way she could live.

The new parents remembered the image of Christ in their home crying real tears before Monica was born. Señor Lopez would put a piece of cotton to the image's face and it would be wet. Many neighbors attest to this fact. "We knew that meant trouble with the baby María del Carmen was carrying," he said. Now they said no to surgery; they would pray instead. "We also knew that if we prayed, our Lord would help us," Señor Lopez said. Help them He did, for the next morning the astounded doctors declared the baby normal and healthy. The blockage had opened during the night.

One evening when she was four years old, Monica kissed her mother and father good night, said her prayers, and went to bed. Her older brother Fernando opened her bedroom door and stood there in shock. A large man, shining as if he were made out of light, was standing near Monica's bed and looking down at her. Fernando raced to tell his father what he had seen, and the two went carefully toward Monica's door, prepared to attack the stranger. Señor Lopez recalls seeing the figure, "but as I watched, he began to diminish and became a small circle of light that landed on Monica's forehead and then vanished.

The girl loved to go to church and hear Mass. She would pray instead of play. News travels fast in a Mexican neighborhood, and the story of the luminous visitor made the little girl a celebrity. On Good Friday, 1964, when she was six years old, she and a group of family and neighbors were praying together in a corner of the house that had been converted into a sanctuary. Suddenly Monica began to gasp for breath and slumped over in her chair. To the astonishment of everyone present, a white smoky substance came out of her nose and mouth and through her dress from her solar plexus. The smoke rose into the air above her, then slowly formed the figure of a large man with a short beard. He was wearing a tunic over one shoulder. The other shoulder was bare.

"The room was filled with a terrible force," Señor Lopez remembers, "and the pictures on the wall began to shake. Two women fainted, but everyone else stood still, fascinated with this incredible apparition. To all of us, and there were thirty-seven people in the room, the figure looked like Jesus Christ. One man had a camera with him, he wanted to have his picture with Monica, and he took a picture of the figure. The figure lasted about five minutes and then faded like smoke. I picked up my daughter and carried her to the sofa. It was then that I noticed her feet. She had taken off her shoes before the service began, and the soles of her feet were covered in blood. On the rug, where she had been sitting, was a huge bloodstain. It was still sticky. In fact, it stayed fresh for about six weeks after that. In the middle of the stain were two large thorns. I have never seen thorns so large in Mexico. I saved them and wrapped them in a white silk cloth."

There was no question in the mind of anyone there about the apparition. It had been Jesus Christ. He had come to visit His chosen one on that very special holy day. Then they all noticed a sweet aroma in the room like a bouquet of fresh flowers. It was coming from Monica's open mouth. They all signed a paper as testimony to what they had seen.

A few days later Monica told her family, "God has spoken with me again. He has asked me to work for the human race. I must show them how to be good. I must show them how to live in love and peace."

At the ceremony of her first communion, she began to speak in a loud and strange voice. "I ask you, Lord, on this, the happiest day of my life, to pray for all those who suffer, for all the sick, for the anguished, for all those who need you. And I ask you also, Lord, that the men of this planet cease being evil to one another, for that is the only way we can stop the wars and the killings." Then the voice of the six-year-old girl returned and she burst into tears, collapsing against the railing in her white dress.

The crowds began to appear at Monica's door. Everyone wanted to see the "little saint," and most of them had physical problems that medical doctors couldn't (or wouldn't) cure. The ill waited for hours in the hot sun just to have Monica touch them. Each time she did, her eyes would fill with tears and she would call upon Jesus to bring about a miracle. Seldom did He fail her. Literally thousands of letters and cards, tied into bundles at the far end of her chapel, testify to the healings that have been accomplished through her.

One day a man with horrid boils and open sores on his face stopped Monica on her way to school. He unwrapped the rag from around his head and a few of the scabs stuck to it. With pus streaming down his cheeks he asked Monica to heal him. While several onlookers turned away in disgust, the child reached up and kissed the man's face. Three days later he appeared at her home. He no longer needed to hide behind the rag. The sores and blisters were gone.

One day a man appeared in the Lopez front yard and asked for Monica. He told her he had a problem and opened his coat. There, cut deeply into his chest, was an enormous festering hole. The man was a leper and he asked to be healed. Monica put her small hand directly on the wound and prayed. Four days later he returned to show her his chest. The hole was gone. There wasn't even a scar as to where it had been.

Another man was dying in a Mexico City hospital. The doctors had told his family he had a few hours left, and they had better start asking around for a good price on a funeral. The family decided to take him home so he could die in peace. On the way home they stopped to see Monica and asked her to pray for the man. Four days later the dying man walked in Monica's chapel to thank her personally. He's still alive.

The testimonial case histories go on endlessly. A five-year-old boy who had fallen from a high apartment window was in a coma. He hadn't spoken for two weeks. When Monica touched him, he opened his eyes and smiled. The next day he was talking and eating.

Señora María del Viega wrote that her sister was dying

and the doctors' medicines didn't help at all. One morning about 6:00 A.M., as she was keeping vigil beside her sister's bed, Monica walked into the room. The girl told the woman what medicines were needed and left with her to go to the pharmacy. On their way Monica turned a corner and disappeared. The woman bought the medicine and her sister got well. When she went to thank Monica, the girl was surprised. She had never seen the woman before, she said, and was sound asleep in her own bed at the time she had supposedly visited her.

I had been invited to see Monica one Sunday morning. It was the first Sunday of August 1975. Monica has her own chapel and has Mass said in it the first Sunday of every month. The services are open to the public.

The chapel is, in reality, a garage attached to the small house in which the Lopez family has lived for the past few years. Señor Lopez works for the National Pawn Shop and earns a modest salary. It just manages to pay the expenses for the ten children in his family. (Monica was the seventh child to live. Four others have died.) "Monica won't take one centavo for her work," he told me, "so when she wanted to have a private chapel built onto the house, I told her there was no money. She went out and for the first time in her life, bought a lottery ticket. She told me, 'Papa, this ticket will win and build our chapel.' It did."

The chapel walls are painted an off-white and there is a beige rug on the floor. Decorating the walls are several large pictures of saints, plus a huge oil painting of St. Francis helping Christ from the cross. In one corner is a pile of crutches, braces, and orthopedic shoes that were needed when their wearers entered the chapel but discarded after Monica had prayed for them. The table behind the altar abounds with fresh flowers and images of various saints. It also holds a large wooden statue of the seated Christ wearing a red velvet robe and a crown that looks like the one the kings of England wear. He sits on a platform under a canopy of gilded wood. The altar itself is a long waist-high table with a lace cloth and a Bible on it.

Mass was said by her spiritual mentor, a Catholic priest who needed a shave. I noticed that even though the ceremony of offerings was said, nobody passed the basket. Monica is quite firm about not receiving money for her talents. (A wealthy Mexican was brought back from near death by her touch, and when he offered to buy her a round trip air ticket to Rome, she refused. She wants to visit Rome but not under those conditions.)

There were about fifteen people at Mass that morning, not counting Monica and her family, who stood in the doorway. When it was over, most of the faithful went away, but a few stayed on to tell her of "miracles" that had happened to them.

Señora María Guadeloupe Fernandez was bursting with energy. For over five years she had been sick in bed. She had lost weight, couldn't keep anything in her stomach, and suffered from pains in her spine and lungs. Finally her husband heard about Monica and came to see her. Monica gave him a small bottle of water that she had blessed. María Guadaloupe drank the water and "there was a rushing and cracking sound inside my body. Everything was shaking as if it was falling into place. In a few minutes, a wave of energy pushed through me and I got up out of bed. My pains were gone, my entire body was renewed. Today I walked from the bus stop [which is about ten blocks away from Monica's home] ahead of my family. We are here to testify what you've done for me." Several people with her shook their heads and declared that what she had said was true.

Then her husband spoke up. "Because my wife was always so ill, I never had a chance to study for my university degree. It was difficult for me even to attend classes on a regular basis. To pay for her medicines, I had to take two jobs and run home as often as I could to make sure she was all right. After my wife was cured, I came to see Monica and told her that the most important thing in the world for me was to pass my exams so I could become a teacher. Monica told me to take the examinations and she would pray for me.

"I wasn't sure that the university would allow me to take them because I'd missed so many classes, but I went there on exam day anyway and a young man said he would overlook my poor attendance record. He also said the first exam, on the history of philosophy, was beginning in ten minutes. Now, I hadn't studied this subject for fifteen years, but when I sat down the answers just seemed to come to me. I got a 10, the highest grade of anyone in the class."

Three hours later he had to take the Spanish grammar exam. From a possible 10 he got an 8. That was immediately followed by a written exam in chemistry. He had never studied chemistry, but he got an 8. Then came geo-history of the world, another subject he had never studied, and again answers "just came" to him. Again an 8 from a possible 10. The last examination was on Greek philosophers. He passed with an 8.

"Here are my papers," he said and handed them to Monica. "I want you to have them because you are responsible for my success. I promise you that as soon as I get an afternoon teaching job, I will open a classroom in my home and teach for free young boys who can't afford to pay to go to school. I make that promise to you."

Monica smiled. "That's why Jesus granted you your desire. He knew if he helped you, you would help others."

I pointed to a picture of Monica on the wall. It showed her dressed in white, her eyes closed and holding up her left hand, which was brightly blurred. "That was taken in this chapel one Sunday," her father said. "Monica went into trance and asked for a bowl of water. When I brought it, she put her left hand into the water. But when she took it out, instead of it being wet, her entire hand was engulfed in white flames. A newspaper photographer who had been assigned to do a skeptical article on Monica snapped the picture. After it was over, he was shaking so badly he couldn't take any more. He was made into a believer that day."

Others had been made into believers one afternoon in

mid-1974 when Monica came home from school. It was the same as every day, crowds waiting outside her house lining the sidewalk and going around the corner just to get a glimpse of her on her way to or from school. This afternoon as she touched and blessed the multitude, she rose about six feet off the ground and, in this state of levitation, walked to her front gate. As the gate opened, she lowered to the sidewalk and went inside. Over eighty-five people signed a paper saying they had witnessed this "miracle." Monica doesn't remember levitating at all.

I asked her if she had any trouble with her schoolmates. She said that because she's grown up with them they take her for granted and never treat her differently from the others. Does she plan to enter the Church? Perhaps become a nun?

"I have been asked that many times. No. I do not plan to make the Church my life's work. I want to study medicine and see if I can help more people that way. There are many ways to serve, and not all of them mean being part of the Church."

The Church is well aware of Monica and when she was six years old gave her a priestly interrogation that lasted for hours. The girl answered every question to their complete satisfaction. The opinion of the Archbishop of Mexico's vicar general, The Rev. Bishop Francisco Orozco Lomelin, is that "while the Monica case is quite interesting, we must study it in the most minute detail. We plan to nominate a commission to investigate all the facts and information. We cannot consider, now, if she is a saint or not. As you know, the Church doesn't take into consideration the miracles that a person performs in life, but rather those that have happened after a person's death. We need medical certificates to attest that extraordinary healings have actually taken place. We cannot give any opinion on the Lopez girl that might influence the Catholic population of Mexico."

I asked Monica to describe the figure she claims is Jesus Christ. She says she has seen him five times, separate and apart from the ectoplasmic materialization that took place when she was six.

"He is a big man," she said. "He has light brown eyes and long brown hair. He wears a short brown beard that comes only to his collarbone. His face is round like a full moon and tanned. He has a strong voice, but it is also very soft. His hands are scarred where the nails were hammered into them and his feet . . . oh, his feet . . . they are the worst! When I see those feet . . ." and she started to cry. Tears welled up and ran down her cheeks. She did nothing to stop them. "He is such a beautiful and wonderful man. Look what we have done to him!"

# 7.
# The
# Pre-Columbian
# Tradition

For all of its centuries of domination and dogma, the Catholic Church has been monumentally unsuccessful in erasing tribal rituals and chasing out paganism. Some say lack of communication and transportation has delayed a complete Christian conversion. I think it's the character of the Mexican himself: strong, proud of his heritage, and knowing that his father's pagan gods worked to help his daily life far more than the imported plaster statues ever have.

It is a fact that the Indian is closer to nature and is closer to the natural forces that control his life. When your very existence depends upon seeds, sun, and rain, you become more aware of nature and her laws. When you spend hours tending animals on a hillside, you get to the point where you *understand* the animals. When your vocabulary is limited, you learn to communicate with gestures and thoughts. When night falls and there is no radio, television, or books, then you listen to the conversation of others and learn about ghosts and spirits and how to deal with the supernatural forces out there in the dark.

The belief that man is controlled or at least influenced by the spirit realm is not unique to the Indians of Mexico. All "primitive" cultures have paid homage to the supernatural. Yet the Mexican Indian, living in isolated pockets of one of the world's most rapidly advancing industrial nations, still builds his life around the ancient ideas of his ancestors. In many places nothing has changed since the coming of the Spanish except lip service to a Sunday Mass and a statue of the Virgin Mary called by a pagan name.

In the dusty desert area of the Sierra Madre live the Tarahumara Indians. Even though their territory in Chihuahua State is just a few hours' drive from the United States, they remain one of the largest and most primitive peoples in North America. About fifty thousand of them, in small scattered family groups, dwell in the forbidding mountains. In the early 1600s the Spanish Jesuits founded a mission in the area and hoped to convert the tribespeople to Christianity. They gave them a church, some music, rituals, and images. The Indians accepted it all and added it to what they already had. The good padres hardly recognized their Christian practices by the time the Tarahumaras had fully incorporated them into their own.

Their biggest celebration is saved for Easter week.

While on the surface it appears they are commemorating Christ's crucifixion and resurrection, they are in reality giving their all to Tata Dios, their god of the sky and the rain.

On the Wednesday before Easter Sunday they arrive from all points, some walking as much as forty miles to get to the small church of Basiguare. They approach the village playing reed flutes and beating on thin drums of cowhide that have been dyed and painted with age-old symbols. Most of them head for the caves around the village, where the women set up housekeeping.

The next day, Thursday, the men construct twelve arches made from small pine trees. These are set up around the outside of the church; they are supposed to represent the Twelve Stations of the Cross. Some men carry home-made wooden swords representing Roman soldiers, while others wear hats decorated with turkey feathers to represent (for some reason) the early Christians. All their clothes are new for the occasion. New white cloth bands wrapped twice around their dark heads are left hanging down their backs almost to their waists. New long-sleeved shirts of various bright colors with small flower designs and new cream-colored loincloth skirts stop just above their knees.

Around and around the church they go, forced on by the incessant drumming. Their leaders prod the laggers with long sticks. It is not a dance of joy, but an obligation of penance. Every now and then a group of the dancers will enter the dark adobe church and kneel before the simple white mud altar where generations of candle smoke have almost blackened the paintings of the Spanish saints. The dance continues far into the night, until the warriors finally pull away and drop from exhaustion.

But at dawn on Friday the drums and flutes resume their steady dirge, and the men form a procession behind their leaders. While yesterday had been given to the Christian god, today belongs to *theirs*. The men have changed their physical appearance. They have smeared their naked legs with white paint and daubed red lines and circles on top of this whiteness. The red paint looks as if they have cut their legs on a thousand thorns. The same white paint has been smeared on their faces, and their dark eyes peer out of this mask, framed by their short black hair. They go around the church again, but this time it is a dance of joy, not of necessity.

In the afternoon their head priest, their shaman, appears with a huge earthenware jug. (It is interesting to observe that on this day no Catholic priest can be seen in the area.) He dips a gourd into the jug and brings it out filled with corn liquor, now ready to drink after only three days of fermentation. He tosses some of the liquid in all four directions, then tosses a full gourd of it into the air for Tata Dios. Then he asks the god's blessing and thanks him for the rain he sent in the past twelve months that made the corn grow. The warriors add their thanks, too. Then, all smiles, the men line up and are given a drink from the jar. That night, in their caves and visiting old friends from other villages, the men consume all the corn liquor available. And there's always lots of it.

The next day, Saturday, finds not too many men with heads on tight enough to continue the dancing. Most are content to sleep off the corn liquor and wait to see if the straw figure has been found. For the previous night, during the drinking, a group of elders has made a man out of straw and hidden him someplace in the mountains. In the morning other men, designated as "soldiers," go out and search for this figure. When they find it and bring it back to the village, the Indians wrestle with it (and with each other) until they decide it's time to carry it to the church-yard. There the grass man is shot full of arrows, is stoned, torn to shreds, and then burned.

The Catholic padres like to say that this straw figure represents Judas and that the warriors destroy him in revenge for what he did to Christ. But in reality, the figure represents their god Tata Dios. Why destroy their god? Because even though he gave them rain and corn last year he must be destroyed so he will be reborn again as this year's fresh crops. Only by being destroyed will he renew himself. Then after attending to tribal business like marriages, criminal punishments, and divorces, the Tarahumaras trudge out of the village and back to their own small farms scattered in the mountains.

Easter Sunday is over. Tomorrow they will plant the next crop of corn.

The autobus from Mexico City to Uruapan takes a

grueling eight and a half hours. For some reason, buses made in Mexico are not built with long American legs in mind, and mine ached from being squeezed by the tilted seatback in front of me. Even before we left the bus station, the fat man slammed his seat into the reclining position and then slept all the way to Uruapan. My thoughts of him were not the most charitable, I must admit.

But the scenery along the way was worth the torture. We left the high smog-filled capital city and drove through several small towns until we hit Morelia, the capital city of Michoacan State. Then we began to climb. The dry plains began to turn into green hills. Palms became mingled with pines until, when we finally reached the high mountains, we were wrapped in white misty rain clouds which didn't quite hide the tops of the pine trees or the tops of the volcanos. As the bus stopped to pick up passengers and let others off, I saw a change in the people as well. They seemed taller, their skin more olive, and their bearing more regal. The women wore their hair in thick braids, either wrapped around their heads or hanging behind in one giant pigtail. Their pleated skirts of dark blue or jet black came to their ankles. Their white blouses, embroidered with red flowers at the neckline, peeked from under their dark woven shawls. The men wore dark shirts and dark trousers. Some had bright handkerchiefs around their necks, others chose to put their spot of color in a tightly wrapped waist-band. They dressed in heavy ponchos, their heads sticking out as the dark woven wool wrapped around their bodies and gave them warmth. They all wore the same open-weave sandals and the same large-brimmed white straw hats with small colored tassels hanging from the front. The higher we got, the colder it became, and I wished that I had been dressed as warmly as they were. And I wished I could have looked as good in those clothes as they did.

The people were Mexicans, of course, but also mem-bers of the Tarascan tribe: proud, fierce, one of the last great cultures to be dominated by the Spanish. Their assurance of their heritage was in their very posture. Their pride was in their walk. Their friendliness was in their warm smiles and their sparkling dark eyes.

It was nighttime when we first saw the lights of the city twinkling through the rain clouds on the mountaintop. Uruapan sits at 5,500 feet and its population is somewhere around seventy thousand. Its colonial buildings dominate the more modern ones. Every road leads into the main plaza, where the music of band concerts vies with the tolling of the two ancient churches across the street and where young men stroll and watch young ladies who pretend they don't know they are being watched.

I had come to this town to see the festival of St. John the Baptist. I was told it was a small but highly authentic Indian celebration. Other towns closer to Mexico City were also having their St. John the Baptist Day, but this one intrigued me. I felt it would be more than worth the effort to see it. It was.

The church dedicated to St. John is not one of the more impressive ones in town; in fact, it is an insignificant brick, plaster, and brown paint building that will never win any prize for colonial originality. The one-floor church, about as big as a movie house in a small American town, is decorated with the usual plaster Stations of the Cross and a large but rather new statue of the Virgin Mary. The seats are benches tilted on end once a day when the stone floor is watered and swept. The image of the crucified Christ that hangs against a piece of red velvet directly behind the altar is not impressive either. Nor is the statue of St. John the Baptist, which sits in its honored niche up near the ceiling.

On the 24th of June, the church opened its doors for an 8:00 A.M. Mass in honor of John the Baptist. In all fairness, the church was filled to seating capacity (possibly one hundred), while a few others stood outside and listened to the priest over a loud speaker. Two nuns bristled about, trying to keep the children together so that they could be presented at the altar for a special blessing.

Someone shot off a few firecrackers. That afternoon a rather bedraggled mariachi band played in the churchyard, and there was some dancing that evening. I wandered around among the few people who bothered to show up, wondering what it was about this festival that had been worth my visit. Nothing! In disgust I decided to go back to Mexico City on the first morning bus. I raised my camera to take just any shots to end the roll, when an old woman grabbed my arm. "Don't waste your film," she said softly. "Tomorrow is a better day." She walked away. I decided that I'd stay on after all.

The following morning, the scene in front of the small church was vastly different from that of the previous day. Now there were street vendors selling popcorn, watermelon slices, chicken tacos, cotton candy, soft drinks, and some small bagel-like breads specially baked for that day. On the side of the pitted and dusty street opposite the church, a woman had set up a game of chance. If you rolled three small hoops and had them fall on three bottle caps painted the same color, you won five pesos. A man sitting on a kitchen chair had the old shell game going strong. Two others set up a rifle range, and if you knocked over a certain number of small animals (painted white and molded from heavy lead) you won a prize.

People were everywhere, dressed in their best and tugging assorted children by the hand. One of the most notable things about Mexico is the incredible number of children everywhere. It seemed population control hadn't reached Uruapan as yet, but then no matter how many a mother had on her hands (and even when she had another inside her) she showered affection and love on them all. The children raced up and down the stone steps that led from the street into the churchyard, while their elders sat and talked or stood in clusters visiting one another.

A car down the hill and out of view began honking angrily. The honking continued as a pair of oxen trudged up the street and stopped in front of the church. The automobile swerved around them and raced away. The children became excited, for these animals were the first of the celebrants to arrive. Their owner, a dark man in light-colored shirt and trousers, had decorated their horns and the wooden yoke that held them together with large crepe-paper flowers. He had also strung colored ribbons around their large necks. And as a touch, he'd given himself a couple of paper flowers for his white sombrero.

It wasn't long before several more pairs of decorated oxen arrived, each cheered by the children. Then several pairs of donkeys appeared, their short manes entwined with paper flowers and ribbons, their male riders also decorated with bright-colored paper streamers.

Then the dancers began to show up and formed conversation circles while they waited for the parade to begin. There were about ten girls, all in their teens, and all quite lovely in their brand-new sparkling clean black pleated skirts, white embroidered blouses, and dark shawls. Their black hair was braided and festooned with colored ribbons. They wore white shoes rather than sandals. There were also half a dozen young men wearing homespun cream-colored baggy shirts and trousers. Brightly colored waistbands and brightly colored paper flowers in their straw sombreros added an exotic touch. They wore sandals and each carried a glass jug or a large gourd container over their shoulders on a rope. The girls had round trays, each with fresh bananas, mangoes, and oranges. The fact that some of the trays advertised a dark beer or Coca-Cola didn't seem to affect their ceremonial significance.

Then a young man appeared, and when they saw him, the crowd went wild. He was wearing a woman's dress, some purple thing with white flowers that came down past his hairy knees. He had on a short brown wig, a pair of battered high heels and carried a purple parasol.

No sooner had he appeared than a tall young man wearing a red and white costume and an enormous wooden head came into view. The face was painted in creams and pinks, the lips bright red. The colored silk streamers and the bits of mirror pasted on the headdress sparkled and caused a great deal of comment.

Someone seemed to take charge, and the assortment fell into line. About twenty musicians I hadn't noticed before began playing brassy music and the entire procession, led by the oxen and followed by the donkeys, started down the street. Most of the crowd—especially the children—ran alongside and cheered them on.

They took a route that led them through the various dirt streets of this poor section of town, a section that was devoted to St. John the Baptist. People called out to them as they passed. Some were offered drinks of fruit juice, others bits of gaily wrapped candies. Old folks waved, children shouted, and dogs barked at the heels of the oxen. It took them almost two hours before they found themselves back in front of the small church. While the oxen and donkeys stayed grazing near the steps, the dancers and musicians came up onto the flat stones of the churchyard. There was much laughter and passing around of the jugs the male dancers carried. Everyone took a swig—old women as well as young men—and the dancers formed two lines facing each other. The musicians began to play, and the dance began. It was a spirited set of steps, the men carefully weaving in and out, making sure that their elegant strides did not interfere with the women's swirling skirts. The boy in the print dress jumped on his high heels and twirled his parasol. The youth in the painted mask danced and shook the colored ribbons and glistening streamers.

Every now and again someone would throw a handful of corn at the dancers and into the crowd of onlookers. Squeals of delight followed each shower of the hard yellow kernels. After each dance the jugs and gourds were uncorked and the liquid inside poured into thirsty throats.

During an intermission one of the dancers, a large young man with dark skin, approached me. He held out the jug and to my complete astonishment said in perfect English, "Would you like a drink?"

100

The sun was warm for me as well, and I didn't hesitate. The sweet-tasting but warm wine went down smoothly and gratefully. "Thank you," I said, "what's it made of?"

"Fermented fruit skins and peelings. It's a special wine we keep for this day. We will begin a new batch tomorrow, and open the kegs only to drink it next year on this date."

Intrigued and refreshed, I asked, "Where did you learn to speak English?"

"At the language school here in Uruapan and also in Mexico City. I live there. I'm in my last year of anthropology at the University of Mexico. I should be there right now," he laughed, "because today they scheduled an important examination, but I told my professor, 'I'm sorry, but on this day I must be in Uruapan!' I look forward to this day all year."

"But yesterday was St. John the Baptist's Day," I said. "Not today."

"Who said anything about John the Baptist?" he asked quickly. "Today is the day of the Goddess of the Rain and the God of the Sun. I wouldn't come all the way back here for John the Baptist!"

The music began and he hastened back to the group of dancers. Again the corn was thrown and the laughter mixed with the sweet wine. Several townspeople had now joined the dancers. One man balanced a bottle of 7-Up on his head, while an old woman lifted her skirt and made quick time with her bare feet as the onlookers applauded and urged her on.

Several minutes later the young man was back offering me another drink and anxious to try his English in front of his friends and fellow citizens. His name was Alfonso Perez. "Professor Perez," he informed me. "I can teach school now if I wanted to."

"Would you do me a favor?" I asked. He passed me the jug of wine. "No, not that," I laughed, "would you explain why they are throwing the corn?"

"This dance," he said, "is to the Goddess of Rain and the God of the Sun. We are throwing the corn to thank them for the crop they gave us last year and asking them to continue their blessing for another year. One small grain of corn can keep a person alive, you know. If that grain grows and produces a stalk of corn with many ears, those ears will suffice to keep life in a human body. We are very grateful to the god and goddess for their protection and bounty."

"That boy over there," I said, pointing to the one in the woman's dress, "what does he represent?"

"Oh, him?" he laughed. "Each year it is a tradition that we mock something that is part of our everyday life. Sometimes we make fun of the President of the Republic. Last year we had someone dress up like a rich Arab that was selling high-priced oil. This year everybody is talking about women's liberation. So we are making fun of it today. That's all. This boy was chosen, and he seems to be having a good time."

I had to agree. "And the boy in the huge wooden mask?"

"He represents the Spanish conquerors. You'll notice that there is only one of him, while there are many of us."

"But," I said, "what does all this have to do with John the Baptist?"

He looked at me as if I were crazy. "With John the Baptist? Absolutely nothing! His day was yesterday. Today's *our* day!"

"But," I protested, "you *are* dancing on Church property."

"Who says it belongs to the Church? It belongs to the people. It is *our* ground in *our* village. And you'll notice," he said with a smile, "that we don't go into the church. We have all stopped at the door."

It was true. The small church was empty. Everyone remained outside. And I also noticed that there were no priests or nuns in sight.

"You see," Alfonso said, "years ago the Catholic priests said to our people, 'You must go to Church on the 24th and honor St. John the Baptist.' So we said, 'Okay, we'll give you that day, but the next belongs to us.' So the next day we come with our oxen, our donkeys, our women, and our wine. It is the day to celebrate the arrival of the spring rains in the mountains. It is the day when life begins again for the Tarascan people. It is *our* day. Don't get confused. John the Baptist has nothing to do with today.

"When I returned from Mexico City yesterday morning my father said to me, 'Alfonso, aren't you going to Mass today?' I replied, 'No father. Don't you remember when I was a little boy you told me never to go to the church on the 24th, but to always wait and go with my people on the 25th?' He laughed, but my mother doesn't think it's so funny. She is much whiter than I am. She has more Spanish blood. She doesn't like the idea of my being here right now, but she can do nothing about it."

"Is she here?" I asked, looking around.

"Hah! Are you kidding? She wouldn't be caught dead here today."

The festivities went on until noon. Then the crowd began to break up, looking at the blue sky as they walked away. "This dance was for rain," Alfonso told me as he sat in the shade and wiped his perspiring face. "Yesterday the Catholics prayed to St. John for rain and there was a thunderstorm. We have prayed twice as hard today, and we hope our prayers bring down buckets more than the Catholics got."

An old lady tugged at my sleeve and said something I couldn't understand. "She's speaking Tarascan with you," Alfonso explained. "She wants you to come and have lunch with all of us."

"Oh, I couldn't," I protested. "This is *your* day."

"So that means we can invite anyone we choose. Right?" He grabbed one arm and the old lady grabbed the other. Together we walked with the happy crowd about two and a half blocks to where the luncheon was being served.

The "dining room" was outdoors on the mud floor

patio of a very humble house. Three long wooden tables had been placed end to end and rough wooden benches alongside them. The tables must have seated twenty-five people at one time, and they were now occupied with men, women, and children eating plates of boiled chicken awash in a dark blood sauce and a generous portion of boiled rice. Tortillas were everywhere, and the spring wine was going down in great gulps.

A place was cleared for us and soon a plate of steaming food was in front of me. On a makeshift veranda at the head of the tables an orchestra struck up a brassy song. Those who were waiting to eat, or had already eaten, began to dance. A pretty girl, one of the dancers who I had admired, asked me to dance with her. I rose, leaving my blood-sauce chicken for later. The music blared, and I tried to imitate what the other men were doing. I'm afraid I put some Brazilian samba and a little rock and roll into it, but nobody minded. They laughed, encouraged me with more wine and applauded when the music was over and I was safely back at the table.

"These girls are very pretty," I told Alfonso as another came to sit beside me.

"Yes, and they are all virgins."

I laughed. "How do *you* know?"

"Ah. Yesterday the girls who danced in the ceremony were all brought to a house of one of the old ladies in the community. It is her job every year. She tests the girls—" and he lowered his voice even though he was speaking English "—with her fingers. They must all be virgins or they can't be in the dance."

I wondered who paid for all the food, and whether I should leave something for my dinner. Alfonso shook his head. "It would be an insult. Each year another family has the honor of serving his neighbors. They save up for it."

They'd have to, I thought. They must have fed over three hundred people that afternoon and from the looks of the house, it was a wonder they had enough money just to feed themselves.

I danced some more and drank lots more (everyone wanted to make sure the Norteamericano had all he wanted) and finally thanked my hostess and Alfonso and headed back to my hotel.

I got there just in time. The blue skies had clouded over. The dark clouds opened up and literally flooded the narrow colonial streets. It rained steadily until way past sundown. I smiled. The Goddess of Rain and the God of the Sun must certainly have been pleased by the ceremony. John the Baptist had come in a poor second.

# 8.
# The Cult
# of The Dead

Unlike Brazil, where I lived for twelve years and wrote the book *Drum and Candle,* most Mexicans did not admit to a belief in spirits that had never been human. Only a few isolated Indians felt that such objects as stones and trees had a spirit of their own, or that an animal could possess their bodies. They said that certain mountains had evil spirits dwelling on them, or that it was pushing one's luck to walk through certain haunted valleys. They wouldn't venture out at night because of the evil spirits that arrived with sundown. Some wouldn't eat a certain kind of fruit, drink water from a certain stream, or wear a certain color.

But all Mexicans believe in one thing: the power of the dead.

You do not fool with the dead in Mexico. You do not joke about them, laugh at them, or forget them. You honor them, give them presents, and respect them. You do nothing to upset them or make them curse you, nothing to disturb their peace and quiet. The dead are all-powerful, and quite often a dead man has more influence than when he was alive.

While the ancients were sorry to see a friend or a loved one die, they did not mourn them. They felt the dead were only carrying out another part of their life cycle. Unlike Europeans of this same era, who dressed in black and felt sorrier for themselves than for those who had died, the Indians of Mexico were glad to see the progression of their friends' souls. The sun rose in the morning and set at night. A soul rose in birth and set in death. The sun always reappeared in the morning; a soul would be reborn as well.

Death was as important a part of the circle of existence as was life and as such, it was to be awaited—actually longed for, not feared.

The ninth month of the year was dedicated to the worship of death. Parents payed witches and sorcerers good sums of money or fancy gifts so that death would not take their children prematurely for another year. The tenth month of the year was dedicated to those who had died, a month-long offering of food and drink to souls far from their earthly home. It was also a time of human sacrifice and bloody rituals.

Blood played a most important ritual role in the life of these people. In their dim past, in the era even before the great floods, there had been fifty-two days when the sun did not shine. The sun had died, and the people waiting for a new sun were terrified. When the new sun (our present sun) finally did appear and bathe the earth in light, the people rejoiced. The sun gave them life—so they gave the sun life as well. The idea behind human sacrifice was simply that if offered blood and beating hearts, the sun would accept this new energy and keep on shining. By the time of the Conquest, Aztec and Mayan priests had so ingrained this idea into the worshipers' minds that young men and women considered it an honor to die so that the sun might live.

Sacrifices were demanded by other gods as well, especially Tezcatlipoca, the god of negative forces who was responsible for Quetzalcoatl's downfall. One day a year ("To my disgust, it fell on Easter Sunday," recorded an early Catholic priest) a young man was sacrificed to this god. He had been chosen a year before, chosen for his good looks and refined temperament. They dressed him in the finest of robes and taught him how to play the flute. He would spend his time walking through the streets greeting people, being given flowers, and playing his music. He was accompanied by eight well-dressed attendants, and everyone he met bowed and greeted him.

Twenty days before the feast day, four carefully chosen young virgins were given to him as wives. Then his hair was cropped close to his head like a warrior's. He was feasted and fêted for five days before the big banquet. Then he was led to the temple and up the steps of the pyramid. On the way up, he deliberately broke each of the flutes he had been playing that year. At the very top he was tied to the sacrifical stone. A high priest struck his chest with a jade dagger, ripped out his still beating heart, and offered it to the sun. It was the old cycle all over again: birth, enjoyment, death, and resurrection into a better plane of existence.

There were various "heavens" to which a soul could go, depending on what he wanted and how he had died. Warriors who died in battle or were sacrificed to the sun god would join the sun and, after four years, would return to earth as beautiful birds with fine feathers. Women who died in childbirth would also go to the sun. If a person died of dropsy, gout, scabies, leprosy, was drowned, or struck by lightning, he went to a paradise called Tlalcon full of food and drink, beautiful flowers, and peace. Those who died of other diseases (considered a chastisement of the gods) would go to Mictlán, an equivalent of our hell. It was in Mictlán that Quetzalcoatl sought the bones of his ancestors, and by pouring his own blood on them, brought them back to life and started the human race again.

From an Aztec chronicle of the period:

*When we die . . . we really never do,*
*because we live, we resurrect,*
*we continue living, then we awaken.*
*This fills us with joy."*

The Catholic priests, however, were not so enraptured by these ceremonies and these ideas of an easy spiritual progression with no purgatory to pass through. They brought in their idea of the grim reaper. Because the Indians had adorned so many of their buildings, pottery, and even their foods with a *happy* grinning skull, they accepted the skull and crossbones of the Europeans. When the Indian craftsmen began making adornments for the rapidly burgeoning Catholic churches, they put a skull and crossbones—their symbol for eternal life—at the base of each crucifix. The priests, to explain this to themselves and their Spanish worshipers, claimed the bones were those of Adam waiting for the day of resurrection. When half-breed artists began creating fine oil portraits of various European saints, they would always make sure there was a skull and crossbones somewhere in the design. Everlasting life, they said. The priests declared it represented "culture and learning" or was a reminder of human mortality, and looked the other way.

Today in modern Mexico, happy death is everywhere. Grinning candy skulls are sold in bakeries, and you can buy them decorated with any name you choose. It's all for the Day of the Dead, which falls on November 2. Most Mexicans believe this is the one day of the year when the dead are permitted to return to their families for a celebration. Tables are laid for the dead, favorite foods are prepared, and marigolds (considered the dead's favorite flower in Aztec times) are in vases all over the house.

Graves are decorated with ceramic skulls, wreaths of marigolds, and colored ribbons. In the cemetery of San Agustín Tecómitl in the valley of Mexico, prizes are given for the fanciest decorated grave. The people set up clay figures representing their dead at various functions while they were still alive (the scenes ranging from office to bedroom), weave ornate wreaths of flowers and ribbons, and spend hours making graphic mosaics from various colored seeds. At some cemeteries in Oaxaca, children accompany their elders to the cemetery at midnight. While the elders pray and decorate the graves the youngsters play card and dice games on the tombstones by candlelight. Other cemeteries have roving bands of mariachis who for a few pesos will play the dead man's favorite song. Then everyone goes back home to the awaiting feast. The dead don't eat the fancy food, of course, but they hover around and inhale the delicious aromas.

All over Mexico, artisans turn out special pottery and clay figures of skulls, skeletons, and people in caskets to help celebrate November 2nd. As Mexican families tend to be large, there is always someone on the other side to communicate with. Private altars are set up in living rooms and back yards, and candy skulls bearing the names of the deceased are placed on it. Tourists are usually shocked to see how the Mexican children eagerly gobble down these skulls when the ceremonies are over.

Mexican children conjugate the verb morir "to die" like this:

*I die,*
*You decease,*
*He, she, or it expires.*
*We stretch out,*
*You get the shroud,*
*They vanish.*

As I traveled and talked, I met all types of people who looked "normal" enough, but whose personal lives were stranger than fiction. Take the case of Ruben, for example.

Ruben is twenty-three. He has little formal education and no great desires in life. He sleeps and eats well. He sleeps in tombs in a cemetery in Mexico City and he eats the food that mourners place for the dead.

# THE CULT OF THE DEAD

"When I was five years old my mother died, then my father disappeared. I had two older brothers and they vanished too. I survived by begging. Then one day I met a man who offered me a hundred pesos [$8.00 U.S.] to help him one night in the cemetery. After all, that was good money for a kid. When I showed up, he had two shovels and some tools. In the darkness we dug up a coffin that had been interred the day before. Inside was an old woman. He told me how to cut off the rings and the bracelet she was wearing.

I remember how I crossed myself before he lowered me onto her body. It was easy. His knife was sharp, and her bones were brittle.

"Nothing happened to me after that. I mean no ghost came and got me or anything. I used to hang around the graveyard a lot. Every now and again someone would ask me to do the same thing on another corpse. I got so I knew my way around the cemetery at night and knew which doors to which tombs were open. Rich people put nice little houses above the ground for their dead—better houses than some poor people live in, I'll tell you. Anyway, I know which ones are safe, so I don't have to worry any more about a dry place to sleep. Oh, there are night guards, but they don't stray out into the cemetery very much. They're afraid of the dead, and besides, their salaries aren't enough for them to get scared to death in the line of duty.

"There is a life to the cemetery, though. Very often I'd see couples sneak in past the guard and make love in a tomb. I used to watch from the little windows they put in the walls. Once, just as the man was going strong, I slipped and fell. I almost laughed myself sick seeing those two running madly across the cemetery, his bare ass under his flapping shirttail and she with her panties around her ankles.

"I always have to be on the lookout for other thieves, too. You can get a lot of money for an iron cross or a bronze door. The best place to clean up is in the tombs of

111

well known sports figures. Their family usually puts their gold and silver trophies in there with them. But you have to be fast. If you wait a day or two, someone else will beat you to them. Often I was inside those tombs before the sound of the funeral cortege was out of earshot.

"Sometimes if I save enough of the wire that holds the flowers together, it brings me a few pesos. But I have more competition than you can imagine! No sooner would the rich people leave, than poor people would show up and put the rich man's flowers on their relatives' graves. Naturally, I don't steal those flowers from the poor. You have to respect them.

"The best day is November 2nd, the Day of the Dead, when people come and leave fresh fruit, chocolates, and even bottles of whiskey. I never feel bad about eating that stuff. I never saw a dead person reach out his hand to take it. I figure they wouldn't want it to rot.

"I don't like nights of the full moon, because that's when the witches come to the cemetery. They are always looking for coffin nails, some dead man's fingernail parings, or something strange like that. The most popular thing is to put a bottle of water on a grave at midnight and then come back for it when the full moon has 'worked' it. I stay away from those witch people. Who would want to associate with them? They're strange!"

# 9.
# The
# Witchcraft
# of the Ancients

Inside a fetid cell in the city of San Luis Potosí, the four women posed for the official police photographer. Three of them, in their late forties, wore dirty aprons over their cotton housedresses. The fourth, the teen-aged daughter of one of the three, wore a white blouse outside her dark blue cotton skirt. They looked like ordinary women on their way to market. Yet they were in jail. Their crime? They had killed a witch.

"Maria Mendoza had to die!" said one. "She was making hexes that caused the spirit of Cuitlacoche to leave us. Before she started her witchcraft, everything was fine, but she made him abandon us and go over to her. Then everything started getting bad for us. The only way to get the spirit back was to kill her!"

"You're not sorry you murdered this woman?" I asked.

113

The teenager shook her head. "We did right by removing a wrong."

"But how did you know this lady was the one who was doing these things?"

"Another witch told us. We went to see a witch who lives up in the mountains, and he told us Maria Mendoza was the one. He also told us how to kill her. He said that we must get her alone and strangle her, but as we did it, we were to cut her body with broken bottles. Then we were to cut her legs. That way, the spirit would leave through her blood and come with us."

The four went to see Maria and found her with her ten-year-old grandson. They gave the boy some money and asked him to buy them some soft drinks. As soon as he left, they told the old woman why they had come. She denied stealing their spirit, but it didn't do much good. The four jumped her, shoving her to the floor of her stick-and-mud house. While one began strangling her, the others began cutting her with the broken bottles. Blood spurted everywhere, and they managed to twist her head completely around.

When the grandson returned with the soft drinks, the four fled into the hills. The police went after them, straight to the sanctuary of the male witch in the mountains. Three of the women were there. As the officers arrived, the witch was going through a special ritual to make sure that the spirits would keep the police from finding them.

Mysticism, reincarnation, astrology, prophesy, karma, fate—these psychic and occult beliefs had been the downfall of the greatest civilization in the Western Hemisphere.

Things psychic had played an everyday role in the life of the ancient Aztecs and Mayans. Their lives were governed by omens in the stars, messages from the dead, readings from mediums, curses by witches, and the fear of the unknown.

The Chontales live high in the mountains of Oaxaca

Gustavo: the best Tarot reader in Mexico
(*David St. Clair*)

The late English
psychic healer
Kenneth
Bannister

Dancing to
celebrate the
ancient gods in
Uruapan
(*David St. Clair*)

Crowds waiting
their turn for a
reading in El
Templo de la Fe
(*David St. Clair*)

Mary King,
Mexico's top
medium (*David
St. Clair*)

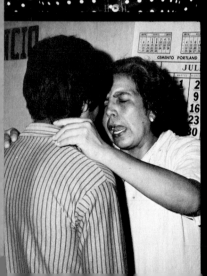

One of the many
mediums in El
Templo de la Fe
who give psychic
advice on an
assembly-line
basis (*David St.
Clair*)

A woodcut by the popular folk artist Jose Guadalupe Posada that appeared in *Gaceta Callejera*, August 24, 1893: the ghost of Pachita the nougat vendor returns to seize the man who killed her

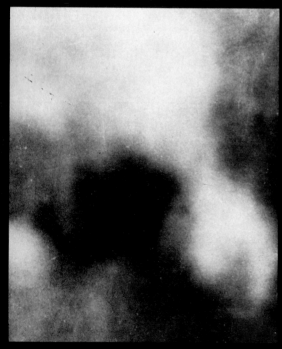

The ectoplasmic figure that hovered over the child-healer Monica Lopez. Some claim to see a bare shoulder on the left, a profile looking toward the right, and the right shoulder covered with a "cloth." The figure appears to have its hands on Monica's head—the white oval near right center

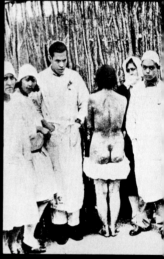

The healer Niño Fidencio examining a patient *(Contenido)*

▶

Niño Fidencio, his weight supported by pulleys, walks across the backs of his patients to heal them *(Contenido)*

The Salazar children of Las Limas with the image of the "Virgin" that they unearthed (*Contenido*)

State, a forbidding and isolated region that few "civilized" men have ever crossed. Chilly, desolate, and riddled with superstition, the area is a repository for ghost stories and legends. The older women still wear colorful blouses and long full skirts. Some of the men still wear the cream-colored loose homespun shirts and baggy trousers of their ancestors. They believe that the trees and rocks have spirits of their own, and one of the worst things that can be done is to offend the wind. You do not blame the wind when it blows the soil from your best farmland or when it brings the rain into your hut. You do not offend the spirit of the river by throwing garbage into it. The river spirit can grab you, even when you are walking along the banks, and pull you in.

The Chontales believe in one omnipotent god, but prefer to worship the minor gods that are all around them. They consider the mountains to be one god and the rain clouds that form over them another.

They have great respect for animals, and while they will kill to eat, they will not kill an animal that they find sick or wounded. They say it should die a natural death and that they would not kill a human in the same condition.

Unlike other Indian tribes, they have a definite Devil that gets them (and himself) into all kinds of trouble. When man and woman first appeared on earth, the Devil saw that there was no way for them to reproduce, so he cut off his lips and tried to make a vagina for the woman. He experimented in placing it in several parts of the body, but it kept falling off. Finally he threw it at her in disgust and it landed between her legs.

After that, it was easy to know where to place the man's sexual organs. Then the Devil showed the couple how to have sexual relations. This so angered the one main god that he threw them all out of the paradise he had created for them. He had wanted humans to reproduce in another way, but now that the Devil had shown them the pleasurable way, there was nothing to be done but let them create other men and women in the same manner.

The Chontales don't think it's their fault that they enjoy sex—the Devil made them do it.

They have a terrible fear of witchcraft and tend to blame a witch for everything that goes wrong. If a child is born deformed, it is a witch's fault. If a cow dies or dries up, a witch has done it. If a husband abandons his wife, he has been cursed by a witch. There are few witches among the Chontales, and it's no wonder. Their law says it is permissible to kill a witch.

It hadn't been easy to become a witch in pre-Spanish Mexico. It was more than just having the desire; only those who were born under the astrological sign of rain could practice this craft.

They even had their own god, Tezcatlipoca, who aside from being the patron saint of witches was also god of the night. In order to take possession of the night, he had changed himself into a jaguar and chased away a rival god. As far as the Aztecs were concerned, every competent witch knew how to change himself into an animal. If an Aztec came across an animal at night, he was especially cautious and courteous, never knowing but that it was a witch in disguise.

Aztec witches could fly—not on broomsticks, but on wings of woven straw. First they removed their legs to ease their aerial movements. Then, stretching out their arms in the form of the cross (which the Spanish padres were also against: they said it was mocking the crucified Christ), they took off for anywhere they chose to work their various cures, hexes, and curses. A really good witch could make himself invisible or could keep his body at home, yet be seen bodily in another place.

Aztec witches were usually men who had been trained in their craft by senior witches. It was a legal profession and a needed one. They were often of the upper classes and were called upon by the rulers and army leaders, not only to predict events but to help influence them. (They were blamed in part for not being able to stop Cortez.) They weren't burned for their sorcery, but encouraged for it; after all, they were working in direct communication with the gods.

Witches caused most of the illnesses, the Aztecs believed. A witch—under instructions from a god—would appear at night and suck the blood from a victim. In the morning the person would awaken and be ill. Sometimes the witch put stones in the victim's stomach or inserted worms in his blood vessels. Sometimes black swamp water would be put in a person's lungs, or his bones turned into twigs so they would break easily. Witches did all these things under their own power. The Devil had nothing to do with it—not until the Catholic Church arrived, anyway.

Even though the Catholic priests tried to stamp out these beliefs and replace them with Christianity and the New Testament, it was impossible. Military conquest never really destroys any people's belief in their own gods. Soldiers with guns are never quite as compellingly instructive as priests in temples or witches in mud huts. Force, no matter how constructive, never drives out supernatural fear. Spirits do not flee from swords, and the power of the dead is always stronger than that of the living.

The Spanish conquerors were not above a belief in the supernatural themselves. Those who came from the Old World to colonize the New brought their talismans and amulets, their ghost stories and Tarot cards, their fear of the unknown.

Transplanted Catholic priests knew only too well the power European witches wielded. Reports from the Inquisition told of entire bands of witches, each more than two hundred strong, practicing in Spain. The Church tried to stamp them out, but succeeded only in breaking them down into smaller groups.

Their luck with the Indian witches was no better. The priests heard about the witches and began to preach against them the way they had done back in the Old Country. But while the padres railed against witchcraft to their Indian charges, there wasn't much they could do to stop it. The Aztecs and Mayans had esteemed and feared their witches at the same time. Indeed, their sermons only gave the Indian witches new power.

The padres knew that Spanish witches could decimate entire families with "the evil eye." Spanish witches could fly on broomsticks, could make hideous potions to drive men wild, and could enter the hearts of even the most pious. The priests divided the world into two camps: those who believed in Christ and those in league with the Devil. There was no middle ground. They claimed the Indian witches were in league with the Devil and this potent god of the underworld was working to destroy all men.

This was a new idea to the Indians. As far back as Quetzalcoatl, man had been both good and bad. The Indians believed that man didn't have to choose but had to learn to live with both forces inside him. Now suddenly here were the padres dividing the world. You cannot be both good *and* bad. You must choose. That's why, when the Church proclaimed it would eliminate evil, the Indians were amazed. One witch, tortured by an early padre, asked his captor how the white men planned to eliminate evil. "Isn't it the same thing," he wondered, "as trying to pull a fish from the water without getting your hand wet?"

Indian witches, glad to have somebody that strong on their side, accepted the Devil with open arms. The net result was that witchcraft in the New World, no longer a monopoly of the native upper classes, increased tremendously.

The Spanish brought their images of saints; the Indians accepted them and put them up alongside the images of their own gods and goddesses. Why not? The white man's gods must be powerful spirits to have aided them in the conquest, to have shown them how to build ships that cross the oceans and to kill with lightning from a stick. Why not accept these gods and take whatever they had to offer?

The white padres insisted that the crucifix be placed on their "pagan" altars. Why not? If that man on the cross really was the son of God, then he was right at home with the other gods as well. Didn't all deities come from the same place? Didn't the padres talk of heaven up there in the sky? Didn't their own priests point towards the heavens when they beseeched their gods for a blessing? During Mass didn't the padres raise that cup to the heavens? Hadn't the Indian priests before them raised up the still warm human hearts? It must be all one and the same thing; no reason to fight it. Embrace it and take the best from both.

The Church set up an Inquisition in Mexico to eradicate heresy from the Europeans who lived there (many had fallen by the wayside as soon as they got far enough away from the Spanish Church), as well as the descendants of the Spanish-Indian settlers. The Church reasoned that having some white blood and being baptized in the Church made a person a Christian. Those Christians were not allowed to stray from the flock or have heretical ideas.

But the pure Indian was exempt from torture of this kind, having been declared, officially, to belong to an inferior order of beings somewhere between animal and man. A creature this low could not be expected to understand theological refinements handed down by Rome. Thus the pure-blooded witch went unpunished. Thus Aztec witchery grew.

Witches flourished in the larger cities where there was more unrest and discontent, where Indians and those of mixed blood were suddenly in the lower social strata. Those who remembered their forefathers as wealthy nobles were brought to the level of day laborers and servants. It was a hard blow to Aztec pride. When arguments broke out among them and hatred became intense, witches were called upon to settle the score.

The Aztec witches copied the idea of love potions from their Spanish colleagues and did a brisk business among the young and lonely. In those days of strict chaperoning and social rigidity, it wasn't easy for a girl to meet a man. Once she had met him, however, she would go to any length to catch him. Colonial señoritas sought advice from Indian *brujos* (they were more powerful than Spanish ones) and paid them well for anything that would bring them the "right" man. A girl would probably be given this old Indian witch's remedy to assure his love:

*Take a small bit of the man's beard, cutting it as close as possible near the ear (if he doesn't wear a beard, then from his sideburns). Take a silver coin that has been sitting in the sun for at least half a day. Put the coin and the hair into a new pot, fill it with wine, and add sage and rue. Bring this mixture to a boil, and after one hour, take out the coin. When you wish the man to love you, lead him to where the pot is boiling and, holding the coin in your right hand, whisper in his ear these words: "Rose of love, flower of thorns." Then touch his arm lightly with the coin. Make sure that this happens near the boiling pot, because the man's passion will be measured by the heat of the wine. Be careful that you don't spill the pot, because then the man's ardor will be carried to the extreme.*

What happens if you don't have a pot to boil wine in?

*Try to get an object that the man has used for a length of time. At night, place this object between your legs and think intensely of being loved by him until you fall asleep. Do this nine nights in a row. Then break off a little piece from this object and burn it on a Friday, just at dawn. Save the ashes, and when the opportunity arises, let the ashes scatter over the man's body. Or get his servant to sprinkle the ashes on his undergarments.*

Men wanted to get into the act too. If there was a married woman one wished to seduce, the Mexican witch would offer the following recipe:

*On the night of San Juan, at midnight, pick a handful of verbena leaves. At the moment you pull them, say, "By the virtue of the goddess of love, I ask you to make Señora So-and-So love me as I desire her." This done, you put the leaves inside your shirt so that they are touching your skin, and you go home. All the way home, repeat the words you spoke as you gathered the leaves. When you get home, put the leaves in a new green silk handkerchief and place it in an airy spot for exactly twenty-one days. Then remove the contents and grind the leaves to powder. Then go to the home of the married lady of your choice. Touch her hands, and if possible her face, with your hands, which should be covered with a light coating of this magical powder. If you are able to do this, your victory is assured.*

Annals of the Mexican Inquisition tell of many witchcraft consultations. One that stands out is that of Don Ignacio Pilar who at the age of sixty-five wanted to regain his sexual potency. He went to a witch and was given a special oil. He rubbed himself with this oil and went into the back streets of the city. The girls flocked around him. Soon, half a dozen had literally carried him back to his home. The neighbors heard the revelry all that night. In the morning his servant found Don Ignacio. He was on the bed. He was dead. He had a broad smile on his face.

The Aztecs and Mayans had another occult tradition that the early Catholic fathers couldn't figure out: a fascination with their front teeth. The Spanish were amazed to see many of the top-ranking dignitaries with circles of jade and turquoise imbedded in their incisors. When they opened their mouths to talk or smile, the effect of the colors against the white teeth and dark skin was fascinating. The clerics doubted it had anything to do with Christianity, and so they were against it.

Of course it didn't have a thing to do with the imported religion. It was a form of protection, an amulet against the evil eye and possession by witchcraft.

Anthropologists have only begun to unscramble this dental preoccupation, but it seems to point toward the God of the Sun. In all the ancient representations of this god, he has his lateral front teeth filed to display two center Bugs Bunny-style incisors. On some statues of this god, archaeologists have found jade and turquoise imbedded in his smile. This god was the most powerful of all. It was to him that the sacrifices were made. He, with his bright light, scared away the demons and chased away the night. Thus the ancients who could afford it (especially the lords and priests) had each of their front teeth, both uppers and lowers, embellished with the magic stones of jade and turquoise.

The Museum of Anthropology in Mexico City has 1,357 such skulls in its collection. Amazingly, the strong cement used in many has not weakened in the fifteen hundred years since the stones were inserted. Few modern dentists use cement that strong.

The Aztecs used the word for tooth, *tlanti,* in many ways and with many different endings. *Tlantia* meant to be powerful, to be in command. *Omotlanti* was the equivalent of having taken the reins of power. *Tlantlaza* meant to break the teeth, but also meant to lose one's reputation. *Omotlantlaz* was to have fallen from the state from which you were or, in finances, to have broken your teeth. *Tlantepehua* was to break someone's teeth or to have them removed from power. Teeth were associated with the gods and with divine protection. A man who lost his teeth lost favor with his gods and with his fellow man. To have a mouthful of jade and turquoise (no matter how much it must have hurt to have them put in there) was a sure bet against the evil eye and other man-made curses.

So it's not surprising that in modern days the Mexicans like to have their teeth on display. Dentists still do land-office business in gold-capping front teeth or, if the teeth can be saved, in outlining each one in a thin but noticeable gold frame. (In Brazil I once had a black voodoo priestess remove a curse from me. I was more fascinated by her mouth than by her ritual, for she had diamonds embedded in each of her front upper teeth.)

Nor is it surprising that teeth play an important part in

the occult beliefs of modern Mexicans. To dream that your teeth are falling out, they say, is a sure sign of an impending death.

Señora Gladys Vivanco of Puebla told me that she awoke from a frightening dream where her back molar had fallen out and was lodged in her throat. Two days later her aged mother died, choking on a piece of tough steak.

Ricardo Igartua of Tuxtla dreamt that his front tooth had fallen out. He remembers picking it up and putting it back in its socket, but when he looked in a mirror, he saw that it was chipped on one side. He told his wife of the dream, and they both began to worry. Less than a month later his young son was hit by a car and had his right arm and right leg broken. Señor Ricardo is sure that if he hadn't tried to save his tooth in the dream, his son would have been killed rather than just seriously injured.

Señora Sara Gueda lives in the picturesque village of Taxco. One night she had a terrible dream. Two teeth from her right upper jaw had fallen out, and one tooth from her left upper jaw had also gone. "All my life when there is to be a death in my family, I dream about losing a tooth. If it is a male member of the family, it will be a tooth from the right side. If the tooth is from the left side, it will be a female. So you can understand how upset I was with this dream of *three* teeth. No one in my family was ill, and I couldn't imagine who it would be, but I worried anyway. Five days after my dream I got a telephone call from a relative in Guadalajara. My sister, her husband, and their little boy had been killed during a lightning storm. It burned their house, and they couldn't get past the live wires that had fallen around the house. You can laugh if you choose, but when a tooth falls in a dream, the spirits are warning you of tragedy ahead."

*Brujos*, as the Spanish called them, branched out and became healers as well. They had long known the uses of herbs and leaves and now added this knowledge to their everyday practices. The padres tried to stop this, but after so many were cured by the witches, the Church took another stand and divided the healers into two groups: the good ones and the bad ones. The good invoked the names of the Christian saints while working their cures. They would perform "European" operations: set broken bones, administer bleedings, and remove the evil eye. The bad practiced much the same medicine, but didn't ask for saintly guidance. The bad ones would use false medicines and techniques that often made things worse. (The Church didn't believe in sucking stones and worms out of a patient's body.)

To counteract the witches, both good and bad, the priests introduced the laying on of hands in church. They taught their novice priests how to do it and brought over amulets and relics of the bones or the garments of dead saints known for their curative abilities. They would pass these items over the body of an ill person, and the person was supposed to get well.

The Indian witches did the same thing, but used a hen's egg. They would pass the egg around the body, then break it into a basin of water. If the yellow of the egg was blotched or had blood on it, the person was in need of a cure. It is said that often when the eggs were opened, small snakes would crawl out, or the shell would be found filled with black stones or dark feathers.

Gustavo, the Tarot reader, told me one day he was taking me to see Conchita. "She is a great healer," he insisted, "and one of the last people in all Mexico who still follow the ancient Aztec methods of diagnosing." Naturally, I was ready the next morning.

We took the underground subway for quite a few minutes and then the cars came up into the sunlight to run along an elevated track for several city blocks. At the end of the line we took a taxi (one of those community affairs that takes on other passengers along the way) until we reached the main square of Xochimilco—the tourist town with the floating gardens, the bright flowers, and the serenading mariachi bands. But the Xochimilco that Gustavo wanted to show me was not the one on the colored postcards.

We walked for a few blocks and then cut across an abandoned field near a decaying church. For several more blocks we picked our way through crying babies, garbage slopped onto dusty sidewalks, barking dogs, and curious stares. Finally we reached a three-story modern home that was still under construction. "That's where Conchita lives," he said. It was the best house we had seen so far.

To get to the front door, we had to walk around an American-made station wagon sitting in the driveway. Gustavo rang the bell. After a short wait a light-haired, light-skinned lady opened the door, asked us if we wanted to see Conchita, and ushered us into a waiting room empty except for twenty red plastic chairs. We barely had time to be seated when the lady reappeared and took us down a short hall and into another room, a bedroom. On the bed sat the frailest and oldest woman I'd seen in a long time.

"*Buenos días, Doña Conchita*," Gustavo reverently murmured.

She looked up at him and a faint recollection crossed her small eyes. "*Buenos días,*" she replied, and straightened the red and blue serape around her small frame. Underneath it I could see a white silk blouse and a pink pleated skirt. Peeking out from the hem of the serape were two tiny naked feet resting on a petit point stool. Her long black hair was braided tightly around her forehead, and a pair of gold filigree earrings dangled almost to her shoulders, a contrast to her dark skin and beaked nose. She reminded me of an Aztec mummy, wrapped in cloth and sitting in a display case in some museum.

While Gustavo reminded her of who he was and of his last visit, I had time to look around the room. It was an old room, its walls painted red years ago but now faded into a splotchy pink. In one corner was a glass cabinet filled with various dolls, all representing the infant Jesus. They were richly dressed in satins, brocades, and seed pearls. On top of the cabinet were three statues in porcelain, wood, and plaster, also of the infant Christ. In another corner the top of a dark wood dresser was crowded with two dozen clear drinking glasses. Some had water in them and eight held eggs floating in the water. There was a large blue plastic bowl with about three dozen brown-shelled eggs in it, and as Conchita gave the order, her two teenage grand-daughters brought two glasses of water and four eggs to the small table beside her bed. This table contained several pictures of Jesus in pure gold frames and, in one heart-shaped gold frame, a photo of Conchita taken in much younger days. Near one of the Christs, a transistor radio played guitar music.

"I am ninety-five years old," she said suddenly, looking at me. "This is my daughter-in-law." She motioned to the lady who had shown us into her bedroom-healing room. "They are building a new house for me." Her tiny arm made an even wider gesture. "This is the old part of the house. They are making it bigger." The feeling I had was that they were building around a tomb, but I didn't say anything. "Did you come for a cleansing?"

Gustavo nodded and went over to the bed. She picked up two of the eggs, holding one in each hand. She motioned him to come down to her level. "I can't get up anymore," she confided, and when he was kneeling in front of her she began to rub the eggs across his forehead, around his ears, under his chin, and across his chest. Then he stood up. She passed the eggs across his stomach, down his legs as far as her arms would reach, and up and over his buttocks. All the time she was murmuring something in a low voice. Then she gave him the eggs. He blew on them, and one by one she broke them and dropped their contents into the glasses of water. She studied them for a few seconds. "There is nothing wrong with you," she said. "God is being good to you."

Then it was my turn. I knelt and she took the eggs over the same route as she had with Gustavo. This time I was close enough to hear what she was saying. "O Virgin Mother," she chanted, "blessed mother of Christ. O Jesus Christ protector of all the Mexicans. St. Jude protect us. St. John guide us. St. Peter watch over us," and so forth as the eggs passed around my body, down my legs, across my buttocks, and were broken into the water glasses. "There is nothing wrong with you either," she said to me. "But then you knew that. Why did you come here today?" Her voice was suddenly sharp.

Gustavo quickly stepped in and told her who I was and what I was doing in Mexico. She shook her head. She had nothing to say. I switched on my tape recorder and she eyed it suspiciously as she continued to tell Gustavo that she was ninety-five years old and tired and wasn't feeling well. Her eyes went back to the recorder. "What's that?" she asked.

"It's a machine that records voices," I replied.

"Do you have mine in there?"

"Yes. Do you want to hear it?" She nodded. I reversed the tape for a few seconds and then pushed the playback button. Her voice complaining that she was tired and ill came up out of the black plastic box.

"That's me!" she shouted excitedly to her daughter-in-law and grandchildren. "That's my voice! Isn't that something?" She laughed. "Now I've seen everything," she joked. "Now I can die in peace."

I turned off the machine, and she looked hurt. "Do you want some more of my voice?" I nodded and turned on the recorder. I asked her where she was born. "Right here in Xochimilco," she said. "I'm ninety-five years old."

"When did you know you had the power to heal?" I asked.

"I was about thirteen years old and a lady saw me in church. She said she was going blind, but in church she saw a strange light around me. She couldn't even see the priest, but she could see this light. So she stopped me as I was leaving the church and asked me if I was a healer. I told her I wasn't, and she began to cry. She needed a healer desperately, she said. She was going blind very quickly and

127

she had three small children to raise. Wouldn't I try to heal her? I was so upset myself that I told her to come with me. On the way home I wondered what I was going to do, and then I recalled hearing about my grandmother who had been cured of some disease by a man who passed eggs around her and broke them into a glass of water. I decided to do the same. There's no more to the story," she sighed. "I gave her a cleansing with the eggs, and her eyesight returned the next day. After that others came, and then others. That poor lady is a pinch of bone dust today. It was a long time ago," she sighed. "I'm ninety-five years old, you know."

She was becoming visibly tired and I asked her if I could take her picture. "My dog has a prettier face than I do," she laughed. "Let me call my dog. No, please, I don't like to have my picture taken. I don't want people walking around with parts of my soul stuck to a piece of paper. That happens, you know. When someone takes your photo they also take a small part of your soul." She motioned for her granddaughters to put her in a prone position on the bed. "You have my blessings," she said and made the sign of the cross in the air at us. We had been dismissed. As we headed toward the door she called to me. "Americano. Thank you for letting me hear my voice. I really appreciated it." I started to reply, but she closed her eyes and turned her head away. Gustavo and I left the room.

Back in the dusty sun-heated street, Gustavo was strangely quiet. "She is a wonderful woman," he said at last. "She sees anyone at any time. No matter if it's two in the morning, she would awaken and see them. It's amazing that her energies haven't all been exhausted by now."

"She didn't charge us anything." I remarked.

"No, because she liked you and wants you as a friend. I could tell. Normally she charges twenty pesos [about three dollars] per visit. That's where the money is coming from to build that house."

"But I still didn't see anything," I said. "I really don't know if she can heal or not."

"Listen, David. Let me tell you what that woman did for me and then you make up your own mind." He sat on a low wall of crumbling stones and began to talk. "About ten years ago, when I was sixteen years old, I lost all desire to do anything. I didn't want to eat, I didn't want to study. All I wanted to do was sleep. I would sleep twelve to fifteen hours a day, and when my mother made me go to school, I would sleep in the classroom. None of the doctors knew what was wrong. Finally my mother took me to see Conchita. She had gone there herself several times and had been cured, so this time was my turn.

"Conchita was stronger then. She was up and walking about the house. She listened to what my mother had to say, and then she took a pair of scissors and told me to lift my shirt. Before I knew what was happening, she stuck the points of those scissors right into my stomach. There was no pain, but I could see the points disappear inside me. When she pulled them out they were bloody. Then she took an egg and held it against the wound. She prayed and rubbed the egg against me. Then she broke the egg into the glass of clear water. My mother and I gasped."

"What did she see?"

"Two small snakes were floating in the egg yolk. They were alive and they tried to get out of the glass." He looked at me, this university graduate, and said, "David, I swear to you this is the truth. Two small snakes were in that glass."

"How did you feel afterward?" I asked.

"Well, she put a bandage on the cut and told me not to take it off for seven days. My energy came back and I felt wonderful. After three days, the bandage came off at school and there was a red scar. At the end of the week there was no scar, nothing. I was cured. The woman is wonderful. She is one of the last great healers in the true Mexican tradition."

# 10.
# An Herbalist
# in Guadalajara

On July 17, 1975, the assistant director of Mexico's public health department boarded a plane that would take him to Switzerland and a meeting with world-wide medical men. At the airport he made a statement that would have caused headlines if made in almost any other nation. Because of the lack of trained doctors and medical centers, "Nineteen million Mexicans are cured by false doctors, witches, and healers."

Dr. Andres G. de Witt's remarks caused no panic or even great concern. No editorials were written about this statement or his statistics. "There is nothing new about Mexicans going to healers," a friend told me. "We've been doing it for generations."

Indeed, the Aztecs had their healers as did the tribes that came before them. The Spanish arrived with priests who healed by the laying on of hands. The soldiers in the Mexican-American War sought out healers in each little village they passed through. Emiliano Zapata went to a healer. So did many of Mexico's presidents, and so do many of the Mexican elite today.

Healers are not particular to Mexico. Every nation and every culture has had them. The British, symbols of sophistication, have always consulted healers. The Brazilians, a wonderful mixture of the pagan and the Christian, go to healers the way other people go to hospitals. In the United States, healing is a big business and almost every small town has someone gifted in the laying on of hands. In racially separate South Africa, authorities look the other way when a white client gets a treatment from a black healer.

The Mexicans see nothing incongruous in visiting a healer. They know there are powers that flow through a healer's body that can help them. They've grown up with the idea that when medicines fail, there is always the *curandero* as a last resort. For many without funds to buy medicine, the *curandero* is the first resort.

Many Mexicans, and not just those in the rural areas, have great faith in the magical and curative power of plants. They will go to a medical doctor and, leaving his office, will take his prescription and have it filled at a *pharmacia.* Then they stop at a stall in the market and buy some dried leaves, roots, seeds, and twigs from an old woman. Like most Latins, the Mexicans believe in "keeping all their exits open."

The faith in the use of wild plants in Mexico goes back to before the Aztecs. When Cortez arrived, his more cultured companions compared the usage of medicinal plants to that of the Egyptians, the Chinese, and the Hindus. Certainly it was farther advanced than any place in Europe. Not only were plants used in the Aztec religion, but the climate of Mexico produced a greater abundance of strange plants than the dry Egyptian delta or the Far East. There are plants growing today in Mexico that do not

131

grow anywhere else in the world, and many are used in rituals or in healing.

The early conquerers were impressed with a huge herb market that sat to one side of the Aztec capital (it is now the site of a government housing development), where strange plants were sold with even stranger claims attached to them. "There are dried leaves," wrote one soldier back to his mother, "that can stop an epileptic in his fits. There is another leaf that, boiled and drunk, eliminates pains in the stomach. Another leaf, ground into powder, stops external bleeding." Another Spanish historian, this time a priest, said that he saw the Aztecs stop nosebleeds by holding a certain stone to their faces.

(Once when I lived with a tribe of naked Indians in the Mato Grosso jungle of Brazil, an unmarried teenage girl was "acting up," and her father tied her to a post in the center of their hut and scraped her buttocks and legs with the dried jaw of a sharp-toothed piranha fish. It was to get rid of her "bad blood," he explained. The blood poured down her brown body and lay in puddles around her bare feet. Then he untied her and she ran into the jungle. I saw her about fifteen minutes later, rubbing her wounds with a handful of shiny, pointed green leaves. The next day her wounds had healed. There were no scars, only thin almost invisible gray streaks where the flesh had been torn. None of the Indians could—or would—tell me the name of this miraculous plant.)

An Aztec manuscript, found in the original Nahuatl and translated into Latin by Juan Badiano, divided Aztec herbal knowledge into six major categories. Two full pages detailed the powers of three plants that were "Substances to Promote Sleep." Those who had insomnia (and you thought that was a "modern" ailment!) were directed to buy certain flowers and herbs and "take them shortly before lying down for the night."

Unfortunately, only one on this list has been positively identified: *tlahcolpahtli,* a member of the *Datura* genus which clings to trees and contains ample amounts of scopolamine, which even today is the main ingredient in many commercial sleeping pills. *Cochizxihuitl* literally translates into "sleep plant," and the prescription calls for it to be mixed with the bile of a swallow and rubbed into the forehead. The third plant, a flower with seed pods, was called *huihuitzyocochizxihuitl,* the hard way to say "very spiny sleep plant." What it was, nobody knows today.

The second section was devoted to "Substances to Combat Drowsiness," but the entries are a sparse two: take a lock of hair, burn it and then inhale the fumes. The other is to drink a cup of water with ashes mixed in it. Nothing like a nasty smell or queasy stomach to keep you awake. Obviously, the Aztecs didn't know about the eye-opening cocoa leaf used by the Peruvian Incas (more cocaine than chocolate), or even coffee and tea.

The third section, the longest of all, lists twenty-two plants as "Substances to Treat Fatigue in Public Officials." No burning hair or other smelly remedies for these important boys! Priests, nobles, and warriors could be revitalized only with sweet flowers or aromatic leaves. Public officials were catered to by Aztec law and got nothing but the best when they were ill. At the first sign of fatigue they *had* to take a vacation, whether they wanted one or not. Some of the sweet odors that revived these overworked gentlemen were fresh corn, white pine, fir, vanilla, mayflowers and a certain strain of pepper.

In section four, titled "Remedies for Lassitude," seven plants were listed, and three have been identified. They are the *tabardillo* (*Iresine calea*); *estafiate,* from the wormwood genus (*Artemisia mexicana*); and the hummingbird flower (*Loeselia coccinea*). These were not to be taken internally, but reduced into a lotion or an ointment and rubbed on the soles of the feet.

Under "Remedies for Mental Stupor," some of the niceties were gone. You drank the juice from the *tlatlacotic* root and kept drinking it until you threw everything back up. To speed up a faint heart, a tea was made from the lovely flowers of the *yolloxóchitl* plant (*Talauma mexicana*). It had the same effect as a dose of digitalis, and an overdose would also have the same effect—death. Another "high" producer was a mixture of the roots and the bark from a plant similar to the cacao tree. Why they didn't use the fruit of this tree instead was not recorded.

"Remedies for Fear and Faintheartedness" made up the last section of this ancient doctor's guide. The Aztecs did not take too kindly to those who were afraid. Manliness and *machismo* were the standing order of the day. Three listed are unknown today, but two are from the orchid family and one, *cacaloxóchitl* (*Plumeria rubra*), is a beautiful and fragrant flower.

In 1570, the King of Spain sent his private court physician to study these Aztec medicinal plants. Dr. Francisco Hernandez stayed in Mexico for seven years, traveling, drawing, and experimenting with local herbs. His book, now a classic, titled *A History of the Plants of New Spain,* listed three thousand different species and presented detailed studies of one thousand of them. He also heard—and reported to Spain for the first time—about strange forbidden plants "that have the powers to alter a man's mind."

A good hundred years later, the Scottish wife of the Spanish ambassador to Mexico wrote a book on local customs and was surprised to see that even the upper classes depended more on native medicines than they did on their own medical doctors. "Much of what is now used in European pharmacy," she wrote, "is due to the research of Mexican doctors and herbalists, such as sasparilla, jalap, friar's rhubarb, mechoacan, etc.; also various emetics, antidotes to poison, remedies against fever, an infinite number of plants, minerals, gums, and simple medicines."

Denny Davis, longtime Mexico City Bureau Chief for the United Press International, told me, "Many of the Indian herbalists have given red faces to local scientists because their remedies *work.* For years the uneducated 'medicine men' have been administering quinine for malaria, ipecac against germs and amoebas, arnica to treat bruises, castor oil for emetics, and valerian as a tranquilizer."

The *Los Angeles Times* man in Mexico, Stanley Meisler, also agrees to the effectiveness of these old-fashioned cures. "Many work. For example, many Mexicans and, in fact, many foreigners living here, swear by a tea made from the manzanilla plant. It invariably settles an upset stomach.

"The trouble with the old Aztec medicine," he adds, "was that magic and medicine were always mixed. Although the Aztec doctors might have prescribed the right herb for an illness, the administration of the herb was accompanied by a good deal of incantation, ritual, and exorcism that, in the long run, received more credit for the cure than the herb. This has obscured the information about the various plants' real properties."

It is much easier to find an herbalist in Mexico than it is to find a witch, healer, or even a card reader. All you have to do is go to a large marketplace in any city or town and look for the piles of fresh-smelling leaves, bundles of dried blossoms, or boxes full of chips and roots.

The Sonora Market in Mexico City is an herbalist's heaven. If there is anything you want in the herb line, you'll find it there, including such objects as dried devil fish and armadillo shells. Walking down the narrow lanes between the stalls will remind you of the hay mow you played in as a kid or of a summer day when you passed a newly-cut vacant lot and the weeds were beginning to wilt in the sun. Except that these bundles and packages and mounds are for human beings with problems that range from a simple toothache to a runaway husband. Somewhere amid the burlap sacks, the necklaces of colored beads, and the small bottles of specially prepared potions is the one thing you need to solve your particular problem.

Have you a pain in the stomach or chest? Then take some rue leaves and boil them, then drink the tea. Have you had a heart attack, or are you the nervous type that could get one? Make a cup of tea from one single petal of the yolosoche flower. It will calm your nerves and steady your heartbeat. Boil the shell of an armadillo and drink the liquid. It will take care of your whooping cough. That long green leaf there: for your liver problems. That dry bunch of purplish flowers: great for constipation.

Do you have a bad complexion? Don't worry, buy one of these mother-of-pearl shells, then squeeze the juice from a lime into it. When the lime juice begins to turn milky as it absorbs properties from the shell, you rub this liquid on your face. Is your problem higher up? Are you getting bald? Boil six bulbs from the tule tree and rub the liquid into your scalp. Works every time . . . they say.

Mixed with herbs and dried leaves, you'll see things stapled to cards, strange little multicolor pouches, round objects on strings, paper packets about the size of a playing card that have strange-smelling powders inside and even stranger pictures and claims printed outside.

It is here, with these amulets and talismans, that the separation between herbalists and witches becomes hazy. For these powders and strange hand-sewn little bundles and bags are the same items used in witchcraft. If you know how to handle the potions, the herbalists claim you don't need to bother seeking out a witch.

In a white envelope with purple ink you can buy "Special Powder to Attract Money." The directions tell you to spread the powder over your hands before you begin any task and "it's very effective."

Another envelope, with raspberry ink, shows an Indian woman kneeling before a large clay pot. A lightning bolt comes up out of the pot to illuminate three rather awesome masculine figures wearing strange crowns. This special sweet white powder is "Witches' Powder" and will "rid a person's body of any evil caused by black magic." The instructions tell you to wait till Friday. Exactly at noon bathe the sick person in something called "Spiritual Blood" (obviously obtained at your friendly herbalist) and immediately sprinkle this witches' powder all over the person's body and leave it on for one hour. Then wash it off with fresh water. After thirteen days of this cure, all the evil will have vanished.

Looking for love? "Powder 13" will bring it your way if you'll rub your hands with it every morning. Do you want to be more agressive and dominating at either work or love? Take some "King Solomon" powder and dust it over your entire body every Thursday and Sunday afternoons.

I have two favorite powders. The first, called "I Dominate My Man," comes in a yellow envelope with a drawing of a Victorian lady wearing only a slip and a pair of black stockings. She stands with one foot on the floor and the other in the face of a man who is flat on his back. It isn't clear if the man is kissing her foot or if she's pressing down on his face as hard as she can. She doesn't seem to be very Victorian after all. "Put this powder on your body," the instructions say, "and you will dominate your man. He will always be your lover, obedient and satisfied. Nothing will ever take him away."

My second favorite, "Lady X" powder, shows two modern-dressed ladies of the evening standing in front of a hotel. It's to be used, says the red ink, "at the beginning of each working night." Instead of instructions on how to use this powder, the makers decided to philosophize. "Who is the greater sinner? He who sins for payment or he who pays to sin? Jesus said: 'He who is without sin may cast the first stone.' Sin is original! Go then. Strong and unafraid. And use this powder before you begin your work."

There are crosses to protect you from things as well. The double-barred Cross of Caravaca (with two angels floating at Christ's feet) seems the most popular and is available in all sorts of materials and in all sizes. The cabalistic Great Cross is there decorated with symbols supposed to have originated in Egypt, India, Burma, Rome, and with the Gnostics. In the center is a pile of bright metallic chips representing the Eye of the World. I bought a cross made from several shining threads glued to a thick piece of something covered in green cloth. The instructions said it was the "true esoteric amulet of the Oriental Gnostic Church" and had been prepared with seven mineral elements to attract the cosmic forces to my favor, with seven grains of wheat to sustain me during the seven days of the week, an Osiris seed (whatever that is) to give me strength in body and spirit, a fragment of blessed wax, plus salt and earth from various holy places to give me divine protection and to keep me free from accidents and sudden death. They said I was to carry it in my pocket during the day wrapped in a green silk handkerchief (ladies should use a blue handkerchief) and I was to put it under my pillow every night. I must confess that I cut the packet open, looking for the grains of wheat that were to sustain me and the fascinating Osiris seed . . . but there was nothing inside but a flat piece of cardboard.

Then I bought another, this one with a fearful-looking idol on yellow cloth glued to a packet of something. This turned out to be "The Legendary Amulet of the Seven Powers," prepared exactly the way the high priests of the ancient Quiches used to do it. By carrying it with me in a little bag made of dark red silk along with three coins and by doing some fancy breathing with it every morning and pointing it in seven directions, I would then 1) be favored with great success in business, 2) win all arguments and lawsuits, 3) come into unexpected fortunes, 4) have fantastic success in my profession, 5) see my money multiply, 6) enjoy pleasant travels and 7) have good luck in lotteries, bingo, and all sorts of games of chance. I decided not to cut into this one. I'll keep it for a while and see what happens.

One of the biggest sellers at the Sonora Market is the "Miraculous Hummingbird," which sells for a little more than two dollars. It really is the dried body of a once-happy hummingbird, now wrapped in gaudy silk thread with only his tiny head and beak protruding. The one I got was encased in bright Italian blue and the bag to carry him in was bright red. The instructions accompanying my little bird show that the mixture of paganism and Catholicism is alive and well in Mexico's market.

"Kneel on the floor in front of an image of Our Lord

the Crucified Jesus Christ. In one hand hold the 'Miraculous Hummingbird' and in the other a burning candle. Say three Our Fathers and three Hail Marys. Then pray: 'O divine Hummingbird! You who give and take away the nectar of the flowers! You who give life and give love to women! I kneel before you as a sinner. I need your powerful vibrations to protect me and my senses so I can possess and enjoy any woman I choose, be she virgin, married, or widow, and I beg you by the spirits of Marmarkall, Gullot, Lucipam, and Bedotti that I will never leave you for one moment and will adore you and will keep you in your holy envelope of silk so that you will give me everything that I ask, my beautiful Hummingbird.''

Mexican reporter Maria de la Luz Bernal investigated the hummingbird cult and became quite incensed at what she uncovered (perhaps because the hummingbird is exclusively a *masculine* means of getting "any woman"?) She was more concerned with the money the vendors were making than in the deaths of the innocent birds. "In each retail stall in this market, there is a sale of approximately fifty to seventy hummingbirds a day. On top of that, five hundred of these dried birds are exported monthly to the *United States* (italics are mine). Each hummingbird has a minimum value of two dollars. Adding it up, one merchant makes about $140 a day in hummingbirds, independent of what is exported, which amounts to another $1,000. Now adding the exports with the daily sales, we get the sum of approximately $5,200 a month per stall, just in the sale of these dried birds. Now I'll let the reader calculate how many of these merchants exist in this one market and he can make his own grand total. And it's all free of taxes. But flamboyant journalism such as this has failed to slow the sale or dim the belief in this dead bird. And it makes me wonder: when a woman comes home with her hair all mussed up and her clothes wrinkled, can she shrug it off to her husband as "The Hummingbird got me?"

I had been told by several people of a man in

Guadalajara who was an herbalist and a healer. Everything they said encouraged me to meet him, so one Sunday afternoon I introduced myself to him at his cluttered and shadowy marketplace stall.

His stall contains reproductions of Aztec and Mayan figures; gods with dogs on their backs, cats suckling at women's breasts; short-legged, potbellied horses; and other deities of the ancients. Aside from the color drawings of Cortez and the current President of the Republic, there is Miss May from Playboy 1974, a beer sign showing a muscled Aztec warrior and an eagle pointing toward the rising sun, and an engraving of the various religious signs of the world: from the Cross and Star of David to the Yin-Yang and swastika. Several other photographs of naked girls line the wall near jar after jar of various barks, stones, seeds, dried grass, nuts; just about anything that nature might produce that could be dried and kept. Inside a cage there was a live crow about a foot tall with a long beak. A baby eagle in a round cage looked at everyone going by. A small squirrel was eating the pulp around some kind of large seed. There was a small brown snake swimming in a half-gallon beaker of murky water. Then the stuffed things: bats, birds, snakes, and small animals. There was a large globe filled with water on a copper stand which acted as a crystal ball when needed. The stall itself was not more than six feet long and three feet wide. One person can stand comfortably behind the counter; two would have difficulty.

His name is Luis Gutierrez Hernandez, and he has been in this stall in Guadalajara's Libertad Market for over twenty years. He is of medium height, white hair, and Indian skin. He wears a dapper blue and white checked jumpsuit and without asking him, you'd never know he was sixty-eight years old. He doesn't look it or act it. I didn't think he was more than fifty.

A printed announcement hanging at the entrance to the stall explains who he is and what he does:

*Merchant in medicinal plants. Stall #767. We are at the*

*service of the public for all types of illnesses, be they light, serious, chronic, or incurable. The many virtues of the medicinal plants here will restore harmonic equilibrium, reanimate the rhythm of lost health, revitalize the entire human anatomy. We have special preparations in Astrological Magnetism, Hydrotherapeutic Cures, Uses of Perfumes, Incenses and Pranic Influences for Astral Cleansing, and beneficial results for the destruction of Phobias and Internal Worms. We give complete analysis about internal nails and thorns and orientation that explains the function of Occult Forces by nonmaterial means. We give confidential guidance in the solution of personal problems and unfavorable moral circumstances. Free Teaching of the 7 Cosmic Principles and Hermetic Philosophy! Your astrological record, the use of the Akashic Record to discover the rhythmic number applicable in the diagnosing of illnesses. Licensed by the State of Jalisco, Guadalajara, Mexico.*

After he was sure I wasn't from the police or the tax collector, he agreed to talk.

"Ever since I was a small boy and I knew that herbs could help people, I've been dedicated to this profession. My grandmother Dominga was a *curandera,* a healer who used natural and occult forces. She could cure almost any illness with her plants and herbs. I saw her heal many people, and she taught me what she knew. She learned from her grandmother, and I suppose her grandmother learned from her grandmother. The knowledge isn't new. It goes back and back and back.

"I was born in the State of Puebla in the municipality of Alscaltingo Vedalgo. It's a beautiful place to be born because it has the hills and the flat places as well. There are many people there right now who are working with plants and curing people. It's not a practice that's limited to just one area, you must understand, but an art spread over all of Mexico. It is popular medicine. People know that certain plants have curative powers and they look for them so they can be healed. Of course, a person must know how to use them and how to combine one plant with another for the best results. You must also know what illness a person has. A good herbalist needs to know the human body, to know what it looks and smells like when it is healthy and when it is sick."

"What happens when someone comes to you for a cure, here in your stall in this market?" I suggested. "Supposing I came to you and said that I had, for example, rheumatism. What would your procedure be?"

"First of all you'd have to tell me how old you are," he said. I told him. "Completed years or only halfway there?" he asked. I said I'd completed them. He then began to make a list of numbers on the edge of a newspaper, quickly, with a ballpoint pen. He looked up at me. "What month were you born?"

"October."

"Uh-huh," he replied. "What day?"

I told him. There was more calculation while the crow followed the movements of the pen as if it were some delicious long worm. The numbers 38, 39, 40, and 41 were added up and somehow totaled 15. Then he counted down from January to October and drew a line through the month of August.

"*Bueno,*" he said after a minute or so, "you were born under the influence of the constellation of Libra, and Libra gets many vibrations from Venus, so your sign is a sign of humidity. You are a person who is nervous and permits this humidity to take over your nervous system. Your rheumatism comes from these nerves, from the cold weather, and from uric acid. So I would give you medicine to cure your liver and for your nervous system. Does that make sense to you?"

I didn't know whether it did or not, but it made as much sense as some astrologers that I'd talked to in the States. "What herb do I need?"

"Several, but I'd write them down for you and show you how to mix them for the best results."

"Suppose someone came to you," I ventured, "but *didn't* know what they had. The only thing they could tell you was that they were feeling bad and couldn't sleep at night and things like that."

"If a person knows when he was born, I can almost always tell what's wrong with them." He smiled at me. "Really. It's simple. Each year has twelve months. Each year has four seasons. Each season contains solar waves of a specific degree and lunar waves as well. We are all affected by these solar and lunar vibrations. So when they tell me their birth date, I can calculate whether they are in a high or low level of vibrations in accordance with the season. Every twenty-four minutes the etheric vibrations change. When a person is first conceived—I didn't say when he was born, but when he was first conceived—the germ that is later to become a human being is wrapped in liquid that carries the etheric vibrations of that moment."

I agreed, but I was more interested in his long-dead grandmother. "Did you learn this astrological diagnosis from your grandmother, or is it something that you picked up later from reading books on the subject?"

"No, from her. She taught me."

"Then this system quite probably was in use by the Mexicans before the Spanish came here."

"Of course. *They* didn't bring it here. We already had it. We were experts in curing with plants before they arrived, and we knew more then about astrology and the vibrations of the sun and the moon than they know *now!* We based things on the beginning and the ends of seasons, not the European months of thirty days. That's why the Aztec calendar is divided into seasons. The Aztec calendar has the vibrations of the four seasons. So this practice that I use goes back further than anyone knows. I have studied it all my lifetime, and I can tell you that it works."

"What was the most unforgettable cure you ever saw your grandmother give?"

He thought for a minute while the crow squawked at a child that had poked its cage with a strawberry popsicle.

The crow snatched at the colored ice and missed it by a fraction. The child sucked on the popsicle and stared at the bird. The bird stared back, furious.

"One time," the herbalist began, "a man in our village died."

"He died?" I interrupted, pretty sure of what was going to come next, but wanting to be certain that I was hearing correctly.

"Yes. He died. He had lost all his physical faculties. He had stopped breathing. His heart had stopped beating. The family called my grandmother and she took me with her. The body was lying in a hammock, and my grandmother walked around it several times, not looking at the dead man, but at the floor. Then she went down on her knees and began to dig a hole in the dirt floor. She took some water from a pot she had over her shoulder and poured some of this water into the hole. Then she stirred it and put her face near it and then filled her mouth with this water. She got up and walked around the body again, but this time she was staring at the dead man. Then she bent close to his face, put her lips on his, and forced some of the water from her mouth into his mouth. At first it ran from between his lips, but she persisted until his mouth was full of this water. Then she took the pot from her shoulder and began to tap it with her knuckles. Tap. Tap. Tap. And she called the man's name. She called, and she tapped the pot. I stared with my eyes wide open, for the man began to move and he swallowed that water in his mouth and started to breathe. It was the most beautiful thing I ever saw my grandmother do." he said. "I was eight years old at the time." He stopped and opened his mouth in mock astonishment. "Good heavens," he laughed. "That incident happened sixty years ago!"

"And now you," I said. "What has been *your* most remarkable cure?"

"Well, the one that I remember most was with a man who was suddenly possessed of supernatural forces. And great strength. He became possessed with supernatural

144

entities and ran from his house and onto the roof of another house in the neighborhood. His family, fearful that he would jump off and kill himself, called me. I came with the branches of seven different herbs and waved them in the air in his direction. Then I walked around the house, cleansing it of the evil that was there. I sent the vibrations of the seven herbs up to him and surrounded him with them. The seven herbs cleansed the evil from his body. The force left him and he climbed down. He couldn't remember how he had gotten up on that roof."

"Then you believe in evil forces as well," I said.

"All forces are invisible, but they exist. Do you agree? *Bueno*. There are certain clouds, certain vibrations, that take advantage of sick people. When a person is weak, whether it be in the body or the mind, they are open to receive these evil vibration forces. They can make them go crazy, paralyze them, make them commit extraordinary things and to *see* extraordinary things. Until those forces are driven out, a person cannot return to normal. The plants drive them out. That's why we were given plants in the first place."

"But why *plants*?"

"Why not? What is closer to the vibration of this very planet than the trees and flowers and bushes that sustain life from it, whose very roots suck up the energy and the goodness of the earth? Each variety of plant is as different as each variety of human being. Each has its own vibration and each has its own job to do. All the herbalist must know is which plant is necessary for which illness."

"Can you call these vibrations 'evil spirits'? Like they do in Brazil, for instance," I asked.

He paused. "There are vibratory *clouds*," he insisted, "caused by the thoughts and desires of other human beings. But there are also spirits of those who have left their bodies. Everyone has a spirit. It's what keeps your body alive and thinking. Once it goes, your body becomes a piece of dead meat like . . . like this beef I am feeding my pet crow. Without your guiding spirit, you and this beefsteak are one and the same.

145

"The human body has many forces around it and in it. There is the astral force. There is the etheric force, the magnetic force, the life force. The mental force, the emotional force, the sexual force, and the spiritual force. And everyone is moved and guided by these invisible forces. A good herbalist must understand which of these forces is ill and when it is necessary to effect a cure."

"Then these forces must be taken into consideration along with the birth date and the date of conception?"

"Of course, and also each season has its own particular illnesses and problems that affect the human body. The time of year must also be considered in any diagnosis. And is this illness inherited? Is it part of this person's karma this lifetime? Or maybe some part of an *unfinished* karma from a previous lifetime? There are many, many things to consider in each diagnosis."

I began to wonder if this "marketplace doctor" didn't work harder at giving his clients a more complete diagnosis than the "educated" medical men north of the border.

"Of course, illnesses can be given by the transmission of germs from one person to another or by outside elements that enter and corrupt the body from the inside. But when a person becomes ill through provocation by discarnate spirits, he *knows* it. He can feel it. It's a different kind of sensation. It's a heaviness and a sadness, and, for many, even a terror."

"But is it possible for a witch to send an illness to another?"

He didn't like that word 'witch' and he blinked his eyes as I said it. "It is possible for a *person,*" he emphasized, "who is under complete control of himself and his surroundings and who knows what a spirit is, to send a discarnate spirit to do anything he wishes. A strong person does not have to be a *witch* to make weak discarnate spirits obey him. A weak spirit *wants* to belong to someone, so it is natural that he would obey in order to belong."

"And the evil eye?" I asked.

"The evil eye is nothing but vibrations sent from the brain of a strong person. But it is not always an 'evil' eye. Good can be sent as well as evil. We have love in this world. It is nothing more than good vibrations coming from strong people. Both good and evil can be sent from one person to another. And they can be felt, as sharply as if they were sent on the point of a pin. The mind force is a creative force. Even God's forces are mental rather than material. And being as man is the son of God, man has the same divine powers as his Father. But man should also be aware of what he has and of the consequences when he misuses these powers. The more positive we are about what we are capable of doing, then the more positive we become that we are sons of God. God put everything on earth that he put in heaven. The man who knows this can radiate these god-powers to others. That's why one man can cure another; because he *knows* he can. There are groups, religious groups, who try to confuse man and teach him that he is low and unworthy, and with many people they have succeeded. They have managed, in the name of God, to block out God from His own sons' minds. They have blocked the powers by telling man he is unworthy to have them. To think is to create and man must *know* he can create anything he wishes. If God created the world in seven days, then man can do the very same!"

I was beginning to understand now why this humble dark-skinned man in the crowded public marketplace had so many clients and was so highly respected all over central Mexico. He was not just a vendor of dried leaves and seeds, but a philosopher, a healer, and a metaphysician.

"When a man lives like an animal, unaware of his abilities and his closeness to God, then his powers are weak. But when a man is aware of what he is and from where he has come, then his powers can be used for the most constructive and beautiful things in the hemisphere. Man is beautiful and man is good because God is beautiful and God is good. When a human being begins to under-stand what a spirit is and begins to use the powers of his

147

spirit, then he begins to understand his own powers. Then nothing can keep him from reaching his earthly goals."

I asked, "Do you have a religion?"

"There is no religion greater than the truth."

"Are you a Catholic?"

"I was born and baptized into the Catholic Church, but after studying it for many years, I know that there are many things in Catholicism that are not in Christianity. The first Christians didn't do any of the things that the Christians of today are doing. The early Christians lived and looked up to their religion. Today Christians are divided. They fight among themselves and, what is worse, they go out and kill in the name of Christ. It is important that a spiritual person study the various religious beliefs to understand religion's place in our human culture. But it is not necessary for a person to ascribe to a religion in order to be spiritual."

It was getting late, and the market was about to close. This amazing man had work to do and I felt guilty taking up any more of his time. "One last question," I said, "and it may be impertinent of me to ask it, but how many years of schooling do you have?"

"I'm ashamed to tell you," he said, "but I only went six years."

# 11.
# Mayan
# and Huichole
# Shamans

Men who could write were highly esteemed in ancient Mexico, and everything about the history and the daily life of the people was recorded in colored pictures, symbols, and hieroglyphics on deerskin or reed paper. The written page, the chronicle of a proud and cultured people, was sacred for it held the heritage of the past and the hope of the future.

One of the great cultural tragedies perpetuated by "civilized" man was the complete destruction of the Aztec and Mayan libraries by Catholic priests who considered the scrolls and parchments to be works of the Devil. At least five thousand of these scrolls were burned in Mexico City alone in the first years of the Conquest. Uncounted thousands perished in centers of learning like Puebla, Oaxaca, and Cuernavaca. In the Yucatan, Bishop Diego de Landa made a name for himself with the ardor with which he chased down these "books of Satan." He took it upon himself to search out and burn anything that the Mayans had written. He thought nothing of traveling for days through the jungle to a site where such books had been reported. He also thought nothing of torturing both men and women until they confessed where the sacred books were hidden, burning almost as many bodies as he did books. The count is not exact, but it's doubtful that more than one hundred of these books survive today. Had more been allowed to survive, we would have had a more complete picture of these peoples' religious and metaphysical beliefs.

While the Aztecs were smashed by Cortez and the horde of invaders and "religious" men that came after him, the Mayans managed to preserve most of their culture and dignity. The Europeans didn't go into the Yucatan in such numbers as they did into central Mexico. Even though the Mayan temples became overgrown with jungle lushness, the Mayan beliefs have survived. Because of their togetherness all these years and their deliberate lack of contact with the Spanish, the Mayans have managed to preserve their beliefs and practice them today almost as they did thousands of years ago.

While many of them now wear Western clothes and drink Coca-Cola, they have a great concern for their fellow man and a great reverence for the life beyond this one. They believe in an invisible world around them, a double world where good is balanced by evil, where sickness is repeated in health, and where each human has another body. They also believe that each human mind has been implanted with questions that have no answers on the human level. These questions, they say, were put there to make us think about the non-material life and to make us aware of our brief mortality. "A man loses himself when he puts himself in front of himself" is one way they say it. The thinking, sensitive, and emotional individual cannot be, at the same time, the object of his own thoughts. The flesh and blood man is one person, the thinking part of man another individual separate and apart. This thinking part cannot be understood by the flesh part, and what is correct for one person is not always correct for another. Each thinking entity is a part of God, and because nothing is duplicated in God's body, each man is distinctly individual. Each entity has a job to do and a position to attain. The human body is merely a vessel for the entity to carry out its work.

Unlike others in Mexico, the Mayans also believe that because each human is a spirit, non-human things can have spirits as well. A tree, a mountain, a river, a stretch of valley, or a flower also has two parts: the material and the spirit. The Mayans respect these spirits and give them identifying names. But because of the duality, a Mayan never knows what is "real." He might be talking to another man and suddenly have that man turn into a bird and fly away.

Corn is both the staple of their diet and a god that controls their lives. To them corn is a real, living entity. It gives them life; without it they would die. Corn has a soul and corn should be worshiped. Corn should not be wasted nor cultivated to amass wealth. Corn should be grown to feed the human body. If the human body is not nourished, the soul cannot complete its task on earth.

The leaders of the Mayan villages are chosen for their ability to grow good ears of corn and their ability to listen. One of these men once told a Mexican anthropologist: "The spirit that you have within you puts himself in front of you and tells you everything you must do and prepare. All you have to do is to be silent and listen to his voice. If you listen, there is nothing that is difficult. It makes you a better leader and it makes you a better man."

Because the spirits are all-knowing, they can be very precise on rewarding or denying mortal man. Why is one man's corn crop better than his neighbor's? Why was one man's crop flooded when his neighbor's received the exact amount of rain needed? It is because the spirits of the rain were meting out exact portions according to individuals' merit.

The Mayans believe in fate: "Every individual has a certain number of days and hours on this visible earth. Nobody knows when his end will come. It is possible to extend those days by doing good to others, and at the same time it is possible to diminish those days by doing evil to others. Human beings are born, grow up, and die because this is our path. Plants and animals are on the same path. The sun rises in the morning and sets at night. There are dry seasons and there are wet seasons. There are good years and there are bad years. The world has always been like this. Nothing can be done to change it."

The Mayans of Chiapas never speak of the world as just the earth. To them it is sky-earth (*vinajel-balamil*). Its various levels are this-sky-this-earth, the other-sky-the-other-earth, and the top-of-the-sky-the-top-of-the-earth. The spirit world dwells on another-sky-another-earth or on another-top-of-the-sky-another-top-of-the-earth. These realms are as real to them as our simple "right here on earth" is to us. When a Mayan dreams, he goes to the other-sky-other-earth. Man can see things on this-sky-this-earth because his eyes are made to see them, but he cannot see what's happening on the other levels because his eyes have not been constructed that way. The privilege of seeing the other-sky-earth realms belongs to the shamans—the medicine men or clairvoyants of the village.

A man has a soul, the force that animates his physical body, but that soul can leave at any time. When that happens, the body will die. Illness is a punishment that the soul inflicts on the body for a wrong the body has committed. The soul cannot carry out its major purpose on earth if the body does things to impede its progress. When this happens, the soul prepares to leave and illness is the physical result. In fact, the Mayans have the same word for illness and death: *chamel*, a verb used to express the process of death which usually begins with illness. When a village medicine man is able to restore health to the body, it means that the mortal body-offense against the soul has been removed.

Mexican doctors have found their medicine almost useless among these people because "they treat our bodies and not our offended souls. Only white doctors who understand the soul can be effective with our people." And because the Mayans believe in an etheric body (the soul dwelling immediately outside and all around the physical body), they categorically refuse to go to a hospital and have an operation. When the human body is cut, they believe the soul is also cut, and no human should permit this to happen to his spirit.

The Zinacantecos, who live in Chiapas State, speak Mayan but are different in dress and customs from the others in the area. A beautiful people with almond skin and jet black hair, the women wear colorful blouses and multi-layered skirts, while the men wrap a colored cloth around their heads and wear heavy woven serapes down to their ankles. They are respected for their psychic abilities, especially healing.

Being a psychic or a healer is not strange to the Zinacantecos. It is part of their tradition that years ago all men could "see what was beyond their eyes and into the souls of others." But today it is mainly the shamans (*h'iloletik*, literally, "the seers") who have this ability. In the municipality of Zinacantan there were, in 1970, 160 shamans of all ages and both sexes. The shamans each have a number and are known by it. The one with the most seniority in the profession (not necessarily the oldest in age) is called No. 1, and so on. When a shaman dies, the others move up in line and take the number ahead of them. It's almost, but not quite, like the system at the Spiritualist Association in London.

A shaman can read the past, advise on the present, and look into the future. He gives consultation on a marriage, on a proper place to build a home, or on a prospective business deal. He is called in to officiate at births, marriages, and funerals and is respected—but not feared—by everyone in the community.

In order to become a shaman, a person must dream three times that his soul has been called up for questioning by the tribe's ancestral gods who live in the mountains. The first dream usually takes place when an Indian is around eleven years old and the spirit of the Great Mayor (Gran Alcalde) appears to lead him to his mountain home. When the novice arrives at this home, he is led into a large room where all the living shamans of the area are seated (in spirit) around a large table. After greeting each one, the dreamer is asked if he wants to become a shaman. The novice always says yes, for to decline the honor means death. Then special candles and flowers and a ceremonial robe are given the dreamer and he is instructed in their use. After the Great Mayor has made the sign of the cross over the newcomer, an old and ill member of the community is brought in and the novice must diagnose his illness. The other shamans tell him how to cure the person. In the second and third dreams he is once again taken to the house in the mountains and given more instruction in his craft. The second patient is always a woman, and the third dream patient a child.

The next step comes when the novice himself falls ill and his family calls in a shaman to cure him. That's when he confesses his secret dream sessions to the man and asks to be admitted to the group of practicing shamans. The established shaman then prays and meditates and asks for guidance from the spirits in that house high in the mountains. If he is given the right sign, then he sends the young man (or woman) who has completely recovered on his own (another sign of his ability) to a bamboo grove where he cuts off a piece of bamboo and carries it in his left hand as a symbol of his office. He is then introduced to the community and his own family as a new shaman. His professional work begins immediately.

The shaman diagnoses in two ways. One is by taking the pulse of the patient and "listening to what the blood says." Only a shaman can hear the words of the blood as it tells of the problems within the body. The second way is to take several grains of corn—yellow, black, red, and white—and place them in a bowl of salt water. Depending on how much of which color floats or sinks, the shaman knows what is wrong with the patient.

Once again, all illnesses are caused by evil. Disease, as we understand it, has nothing to do with the condition of the body. The healing ceremony is then performed in accordance with the evil committed, the most complicated cure being "the great vision" where the patient is taken around to see every cross and holy place in the area. This can take up to two weeks of his time. Each day he fasts on a special diet and at night lies in a bed filled with certain flowers. The spirit, pleased with this pilgrimage and attention, decides to stay in the body a while longer, and the patient recovers.

It is not only in Indian settlements where the occult works its miracles, but in small towns and villages all over the country. No matter where I went, I encountered stories of hexes, cures, curses, and miracles. Most were different. Many were unique. All seemed to have "the power."

In the town of Sahuayo in Michocan State I met an old lady whom three doctors in Guadalajara had diagnosed as having cancer. They had given her six months to live. She returned to Sahuayo and instead of dying, went to see a local woman famed for her occult knowledge. The medium told her to get a rattlesnake, cut and dry its meat, then crumble and eat a teaspoonful of it every day with her usual meals. The lady asked several farmers to bring her dead rattlesnakes; when they did, she skinned them, dried them, and ate them. That was seven years ago. Today she is as healthy as any of the pretty girls who stroll in the town's main square.

I met a lady from a small town near Veracruz who told me how a local shaman had saved her brother's life. "One day he was out playing in the fields. When he came home, his face was red and he could hardly talk. My mother put him to bed and we prayed over him and gave him some medicine we bought at the local drugstore. Nothing seemed to do any good, and the next day he was worse. His breathing was so low we could scarcely hear it.

"My father wanted to go for the Catholic priest but my mother told him to get the shaman. His name was Don Illdefonso. When the old man came into the room, my brothers and sisters and I hid in a corner. All our lives we had heard stories about this old man who lived alone with his cats and caged birds, and we were frightened of him. He took three egg-sized stones, I think they were rock crystal, out of a dirty leather bag he had in his back pocket. He blew on them and chanted over them and placed them on my brother's neck. Then he told my mother to go out into the yard, catch a chicken and bring it to him. She did as she was told. He talked to the chicken, stroked its beak and wings, and the bird became very still. Then he placed the chicken on my brother's chest. 'He will get well,' he said to my parents, and went away.

"The next morning my brother woke up and began to cry. He was perfectly healthy again, but what frightened him was the dead chicken sitting on his chest. The bird had somehow drawn the illness out of his body and had died."

Carmina Torres told me of the time several years ago when her father's cattle started to die in a small town near the city of Chihuahua. "We were not a rich family but my father had managed, don't ask me how, to accumulate a herd of seventeen dairy cattle. We sold the milk for enough money for food, clothing, and kerosene for our cooking stove. Our lives depended on those cows. Then one day two of them just dropped dead in the corral. The next day another died and the third day, two more. My father was frantic and rode all night to the house of a shaman who lived far away in the mountains.

"The man returned with father and walked around the corral. He would stop and sniff the air and scratch at the ground with a black stick. He shook some liquid from a bottle over the area and watched as it was absorbed into the dry ground. Finally he said, 'Aha! I have found the problem. You have evil spirits here and they must be gotten rid of.' He and my father went into town and came back with four hens: one white, one red, one brown and one speckled. They also had an enormous black rooster. My mother and I watched in fascination as they buried each hen alive in a corner of the corral, leaving only their heads outside the ground. The rooster was buried in the exact center of it. The shaman stayed the night with us, telling us stories of some of his deeds and experiences. I was fascinated by him! The next morning, just as the sun was appearing, we all went out into the corral. The hens and the rooster were dead. And this is the strangest part of all, not one of the cows took sick and died after that."

To the north of Mexico, on the western coast in the Nayarit State are the Huichole Indians, noted for their magnificent "paintings," made from colored yarns glued to a board, that represent their life and their beliefs. They are noted also for their complete isolation and independence from any outside (and especially Spanish) influence. The impact of Christianity on them has been minimal. They have forbidden themselves any contact with the white man and consider it a mortal sin for a Huichol to marry a "Spaniard." Their chief gods are those of their ancestors: fire and the deer.

Tatewari ("Grandfather Fire") is their main god, and he created them. He keeps them alive through the sun and nourishes them by shining his rays upon their corn and bean crops. He also nourishes the flesh of animals and the fish so that it can be eaten by the Huicholes. His constant companion is Kauyamarie, the Holy Person Deer. This deity is animal, human, and spirit all in one and must never be killed or eaten by an Indian. This animal brings the right spirits to man while he is alive and leads the soul into heaven after man is dead. It was this deer who first gave holy fire to man.

# SHAMANS

The most powerful person in a Huichole village is the shaman or medicine man. Often there are more than one in each village, and they work together for the common good. Such a *mara'akame* is chosen when he is young and trained into the profession. Sometimes he will be chosen as a young adult when his abilities to see and converse with the spirit world have developed on their own. The shaman is knowledgeable in healing, in divination, and in calling on the spirits of nature to do such things as bring down the rain or take away the winds. He is also an adept in the use of the hallucenogenic mushroom peyote.

Few outsiders have been able to witness a shaman at work, but Karen Reed, a graduate student at the University of California in Los Angeles, told anthropologist Peter T. Furst of a rare (for her) experience.

She was in Mexico working with the National Indian Institute in Tepic, Nayarit, when one of the Huichole women, whose name was Lupe, began to suffer terrible pains in her legs. The medical doctor assigned to the Institute diagnosed it as arthritis and gave the woman some painkillers. Lupe refused to take them, saying that she was about to leave for her village to take part in a corn-toasting ceremony where she would drink peyote mixed with sacred water. She was afraid that the white man's pills would interfere with the peyote's ritual magic. Karen, Lupe, and several others started for the village to attend the ceremony, but the farther they went the more Lupe suffered. Finally she had to be carried in a makeshift chair.

When they arrived at the village, she asked to see her uncle Carlos Rios who was a Huichole medicine man. He placed her near a large fire (symbolizing Grandfather Fire). She told him that her entire left side was in excruiciating pain and that she had throbbing headaches. The uncle diagnosed her problem as coming from a broken promise she and her husband had made to the god Wirikuta in December of the previous year. They had made a vow to visit a sacred peyote place and had failed to do so. That was the cause of her illness.

# SHAMANS

Karen Reed witnessed the shaman "pass the holy feathers over the parts she said were aching. Then he blew all around her and made a sound like spitting. He made some sucking sounds over her upper chest, her head, and her left side. Then he took a handful of corn kernels and blew on them and studied them carefully. Without saying a word, he went outside and threw the corn into the bushes." (Apparently he had removed the illness and captured it in the corn.)

Then he made Lupe promise to carry out her pilgrimage to the land of the sacred peyote. Karen Reed, who had helped carry the sick woman up the mountains, says, "Soon afterward Lupe was feeling fine, coming and going everywhere. During the ceremony of the roasted corn, everyone was happy and the musicians came to our house and played while four women, including Lupe, danced and danced."

Like the Mayans, the Huicholes believe that illness is a direct result of wrongdoing. The soul can leave (or be captured) during the most trivial of illnesses. "A man's soul lives in his head," a shaman told Peter Furst, "because that's where the thinking is done. If one receives a blow on the head, he cannot think. He who loses his thinking doesn't know what to do. He doesn't know if his life has been taken or not."

Sounding quite a lot like our own mystics, the shaman went on to explain about the connection of the soul to the body: "The life force is as if it was connected to one by a fine thread. It's like a silken spider's thread. When one is sleeping, the soul can leave the body. It can leave it and get lost. It can wander around from one place to another, but it doesn't get too far because it is possible for a witch or for an animal that has been sent by a witch to capture the soul. Then the man awakens and he is ill. He doesn't know what happened. Then he calls the shaman. The shaman goes to look for the soul to bring it back. But if he doesn't find it, this man will die."

When an Indian has fallen from a cliff and been

knocked unconscious, the shaman will go to that spot and very carefully search for the soul. He must be very quiet to hear the soul's crying, for the little thing is only the size of a mosquito and doesn't know what has happened to it. Usually the soul is hiding under a rock in fear of wild animals in the area. The shaman finds the soul and catches it on the tips of his magic feathers. Then he places it in a small specially constructed box and takes it back to the village. The soul is so tiny that only the shaman can see it, but the others in the village know it's in there. The shaman takes the soul into the unconscious man's hut and very carefully opens the box near the man's head. The happy soul comes out and rushes back inside its true home. Then the man survives and gets well.

Peyote is a sacred thing for the Huicholes and not to be treated lightly. It is part of their religious beliefs, and the visions that an Indian sees while on a "trip" is to be told to no-one. It is his personal glimpse of the gods who are protecting him. As in the Catholic Church, where one must go to confession before receiving the Host, a Huichol must confess before taking peyote. Their confession is a communal affair, with both men and women sitting around the sacred mushrooms telling of whatever extra-marital sexual experiences they have had since the last ceremony. They must tell who their partners were and how often they had relations. The shaman listens and ties a knot in a fiber for each sexual pecadillo. When the confession is over, the fiber is thrown into the sacred fire, thus consuming and expiating the sin and cleansing the soul for its peyote journey.

No expressions of jealousy are permitted *during* the ceremony, but the arguments afterward must be something to behold. Divorce is common among the Huicholes, and both men and women have often married many times. Surprisingly, a father never worries if a child is his or not. If it belongs to his wife—and if he loves his wife—then he loves and accepts the child.

Sex with other Huicholes is not frowned upon, but sex

with outsiders (all grouped together as "spaniards") is a mortal sin. The Huicholes consider themselves to be the purest race on earth, direct descendants of "the black blood of the Sacred Deer." To confuse that blood, to give one's sperm to an inferior race, is to dilute the race and to dilute the powers of the spirits that guide the race. And "spaniards" have no souls! Neither do dogs or bulls or several other animals. The mule is considered a "spaniard" because it is a bastard animal unable to produce its own kind.

Boys who have had sexual relations with "spanish" girls are considered dirty, and there is no way they can be cleansed during this lifetime. If a girl has had sexual relations with a "spaniard," she is unfit to marry a Huichole boy. When a Huichole man dies, his spirit must go through a purgatory that includes being stomped upon by all the "spanish" mules he has had sexual relations with during his life. He must carry the heavy vaginas of the "spanish" women with him until he reaches heaven. The Huichole woman must carry in her arms all the "spanish" penises that she enjoyed on earth and be prepared to be stomped upon by the "spanish" mules in purgatory.

# 12.
# Magic
# Mushrooms

She crossed her shapely legs under the cocktail table and took another sip of Margarita. "I graduated from the University of Wisconsin, why?" she asked me.

"No reason," I replied, "I just wondered about your formal education, that's all."

I had met this attractive American girl in the United States Embassy in Mexico City. She was a reader of occult books, and after she heard my name, we struck up a conversation. Now we were sitting in the cocktail lounge of the chic Hotel Aristos, across the wide Paseol de la Reforma from the embassy, and she was telling me of her experience with the mushrooms of Huautla—the Mexican Tibet.

This tiny village, almost hidden in the rugged hills of Oaxaca State, is the center for the hallucinogenic mushrooms of Mexico. The village, riddled with caves and secret hideaways, had been "discovered" in 1953 by American scientist Gordon Wasson. He was the first to seek out—and publish in *Life* magazine—information about these dried bits of mind-blowing fungus. He wrote of his experiences under the drug and of the old "priestess" Maria Sabina who administered the drug to him.

Word quickly got around in beat circles that there was this old lady who had this stuff, and the pilgrimage south of the border and into the sleepy village began. At first the villagers didn't mind, for it brought revenue into an area where very little money ever changed hands. But after a while, the travelers began to do things like rob other travelers, smuggle out the mushrooms in large quantities, and spread venereal disease. Maria made a fortune, some say, as did other "priestesses" who got into the act, before the Mexican government lowered the boom. Today all busses and private automobiles going into Huautla are stopped and their occupants examined. Having a beard or long hair or wearing sandals and granny glasses is reason enough for the soldiers—armed soldiers—not to let you into town.

I had intended to visit Huautla, but had been told by important people in the federal government in Mexico City that, because I was a writer, I would not be permitted entry. The Mexicans do not want any more publicity about the mushrooms. They would prefer that everyone forget about Huautla and Maria Sabina.

That's why I was interested in this young lady. She had managed to get in to see Maria and had participated in the secret of the mushrooms. Because she works for the United States Embassy, I'll call her Donna.

"I went with a Mexican boyfriend," she said. "He drove a rather new car, and we had lots of pesos to pay the soldiers at the entrance to the town. There was no problem getting in. I think the ride through the mountains was almost as impressive as the trip I got from the mushrooms. The highway seemed to be on top of the world, and we could look down into valleys that must have been miles away. Everywhere misty fog-like clouds would come down and nudge the car forward. It was icy cold, yet small blue and yellow flowers dotted the rocks and there were clusters of multi-colored butterflies at the base of seemingly dozens of waterfalls.

"The village itself was right out of another time and place. The houses were made of rocks and their roofs were thatched. The streets wound in and around the curves. I don't think there's one straight road in the entire town. Almost nothing, except for a couple of Coca-Cola signs, even indicated that we were in the twentieth century.

"Carlos, using a map that someone had drawn for him, managed to find Maria's hut with little trouble. She doesn't live right in town, but outside of it and quite a ways, it seemed to me. I knew that she charged six hundred pesos [U.S. $48.00] to administer the mushrooms, so I was kind of surprised to see how poor and unkempt her house was. It was a little larger than some of the others, but that's about all. Carlos told me that she had to lay most of her money out in bribes in order to keep her religious practice.

"*Religious*?" I interrupted.

"Oh, yes. Carlos said she considers these mushrooms as 'flesh of the gods,' and each time she gives one to someone, she is performing an ancient ritual. She was a local priestess long before her picture was published in *Life*."

I remembered those pictures. A small, thin old lady wearing several layers of dirty cotton clothes, a ragged shawl over her wispy white hair, and sharp eyes peering out of the shadows of her face.

"Carlos talked to Maria while I looked around inside her house. There was very little furniture, only a table and some chairs and a single bed in one corner. The kitchen, if you could call it that, was in one corner of the hut, and the smoke from the wood burning in the open oven smelled good. Reminded me of when I was a little girl back on the farm in wintertime. Carlos later told me that the reason for so little furniture in the place was that the villagers were very jealous over Maria's success. They had burned her house down twice.

"Maria's daughter was there that day. Sorry, but I can't recall her name, and she became concerned when she found out that Carlos didn't want the mushroom. I did. Ever since I came to Mexico I wanted to try one of those things. Oh, of course," she laughed, "I'd fooled around with marijuana and LSD in college, but they were kids' stuff in comparison with the mushrooms. And that book of Huxley's . . . what was the title? About the mushrooms he ate in Mexico . . . ?"

"*Doors of Perception,*" I said.

"Yes, that one. I read it in college and it really made me interested in getting down here and seeing these things for myself. Anyway," and she took another sip of her Margarita, "Carlos convinced the daughter that I was okay and that he would assume full responsibility if anything happened. That seemed to calm her down.

"Maria had me sit down on the single bed and take off my shoes. I was wearing black slacks and a red heavy knit sweater. She said I should keep those on, since the cold would get worse during the night. I didn't know what time it was then, even though the sun was still in the sky. In the mountains and with that thin air it's difficult to tell what time it is . . . suddenly it's night. You know what I mean?

"Maria sat on her haunches, you know like the Indians do, in the opposite corner, closed her eyes and began to sing. It was a thin rasping voice, and because she sang in Mazateca I couldn't understand a word of it. Carlos said it was a religious song, so I suppose it was.

"Then the daughter came over with an ordinary shoebox and held it out to me. I looked inside and there were the mushrooms. Only they didn't look like mushrooms. They looked like some shriveled up pieces of leather. She motioned with her hand and I took one out and tasted it. Frankly, it tasted like hell! It was bitter and made my mouth pucker. It was also dirty. I could feel the grit between my teeth. At one hundred pesos apiece, they could at least have washed the damned things.

"Anyway, I chewed it and swallowed it and then laid back against the wall. Maria's daughter put five more mushrooms in my hand and ordered me to eat them. '*All* of them?' I asked. She shook her head yes. So one by one I put the damned things in my mouth, chewed and chewed, and then swallowed. I asked for some water, but was told I couldn't have any. I made Carlos come over and sit on the floor by the edge of the bed. I didn't want to lose track of him.

"It's funny, but I wasn't afraid. I was nervous when the last of the mushrooms went down, that I'll admit, but I wasn't afraid. Anxious now that there was no turning back. But not afraid.

"I sat on the bed with my back against the rough wall waiting for things to happen. Maria was still singing. Outside some dogs were barking and a man walked by playing a guitar. I even thought I heard a parrot squawk.

"Then it came again. I *did* hear a parrot! It came louder and I reared back, for the damned thing was right in front of me. Its huge wings outstretched and its sharp yellow beak pecking at my eyes. I could feel his sweet hot breath on my face and when I opened my eyes I saw his red tongue darting in and out. I screamed and tried to lift my arms to push him away. But my screams were only *inside* me. They never came out. I never heard them with my own ears, but I knew I was screaming. My arms wouldn't raise. That damned bird kept pecking at my eyes, and I yelled for Carlos to do something, but I knew he didn't hear me. That's when panic set in. Maybe he didn't *want* to hear me, I thought. Maybe he wants this awful bird to blind me. Maybe Carlos wants to get rid of me. He is tired of our relationship.

"That's it! I knew instantly. Carlos had brought me there to murder me! And he was doing it by having a parrot peck at me until I was dead!

"I managed to get control of my arms and flapped them at the bird, but instead of it flying away, *I* did. I shot up and out of that hut and into a piercing blue sky. I gasped at the suddenness of it and then laughed that I was free of Carlos and Maria and that bird. How wonderful it was to be free of them all! I had outwitted them! Now all I had to do was point my way toward Mexico City and I'd fly home in a flash.

"Except when I opened my eyes again, I wasn't over the mountains of Oaxaca. I was over an enormous city filled with enormous skyscrapers. Some of the buildings must have been five hundred stories high. The sun reflecting on their windows was blinding, but no matter where I looked or how far into the horizon, there was nothing but these skyscrapers.

"The bed creaked under me and I ran my fingers over the rough coverlet. Carlos was sitting on the floor staring at me. He winked and I winked back. He raised his hand in a thumbs-up position and I smiled and did the same. Everything was thumbs-up. Everything was okay.

"Carlos' thumb fascinated me as did his smile. Both his thumb and his teeth began to shine. Not just glow, but shine like those round lights they have at Hollywood movie premieres. Every one of his teeth were spotlights that tore into me. His thumb was so intense a light that I closed my eyes to keep from burning them. Then the bed began to move. It shook one way and then the other. I pressed harder against the wall hoping that would steady me, but it didn't help. I opened my eyes. The shaking stopped. I closed my eyes. It began again. So the secret was to keep my eyes open, I told myself. That's what powered this bed, the movement of my eyes. So I opened them again, stretching them wide this time and Carlos was gone. In his place, sitting at the foot of the bed, was a pile of flowers. Oh, the flowers were shaped like Carlos, but it wasn't him at all. It was like one of those statues in the Rose Bowl Parade. Then the flowers became butterflies and began flapping their wings. Then they flew off. They filled the hut with their bright colors and their singing.

"Oh yes," she smiled, "when you're under the

167

effects of the mushrooms, even butterflies have voices!

"Some of them flew and landed on me. I admired their colors and the softness of their little feet until they started biting me and I saw with horror that I was bleeding from all the pores of my body. Carlos was gone. Maria and her daughter were gone. I was all alone and bleeding to death.

"I tried stopping the blood with my hands, but it ran through my fingers and fell into a pool at my feet. As I watched, not so much in terror but in fascination, that pool of blood rose higher and higher until I was floating in it.

"Then my mother was there. Suddenly. I hadn't seen her for years. She was there and she was cradling me in her arms. I forgot that she died when I was a junior in college. I forgot everything. It was so *wonderful* to be in her arms again! I started to cry. Tears of happiness I suppose you'd call them, and she soothed me and wiped away and kissed away the tears as they ran down my cheeks. Then she began to brush my hair. I used to love her to brush my hair when I was a child, but now the ends of each strand ached as she touched them. The pressure of her fingers on my hair was unbearable. Where her hands held me it was like I was being squeezed in a pair of vises. Each time she kissed me it was like she had put a burning cigarette against my skin. Then my clothes came alive. I could feel the cotton in my slacks crawling across my legs. The wool sweater was rough and brutal against my skin and even my nylon panties and bra became like something alive. I could feel the metal snaps turn hot as they dug into me.

"There were colors everywhere. Everything was reduced to colors and energy. My brain exploded right out of my body several times. It couldn't take the brilliance of the reds and yellows, especially the yellows. They were the worst. Or should I say, the best? I don't know. Even today, I don't know.

"After five hours I came back down to earth. In fact, when I began to realize that I was through with my 'trip,' I discovered I was on the floor. God! Dirt never looked so good to me as it did then! I dragged my fingernails across the floor and enjoyed the taste as I put them into my mouth. 'Carlos, I'm thirsty,' I said in English. And when he held my head so I could sip from the glass, I knew that he had heard me and that my journey was really over.

"May I have another Margarita?"

I ordered one for each of us. I let her light a fresh cigarette and sip her new drink before I asked my questions. Obviously, she had relived her experience as she told it to me. Her face was flushed and her eyes glazed. She had to blink several times before she could bring them back into focus. She smiled. "Sorry. You know, it's the first time I've ever told anyone about that. Except for Carlos, of course."

I was curious. "Aside from the immediate happenings, did your 'trip' have any lasting effects?"

"Oh yes," she replied immediately. "It opened my inner eyes to things that I was never aware of before. You know, things like relationships between two people, the futility of mundane chores, the need to *experience*. You know? It also showed me how unimportant the *me* part of myself really is. This outer *me* that everyone sees. The *me* I show to the world. This *me*, this *ego,* if you want to call it that, is really very unimportant in the overall plan of things. There is an *inner* me that is much more important, much more vital to my personal and *spiritual* survival. The body isn't everything. In fact, it's nothing. Really, it's nothing. And all this," and she swept her arms around the room, "all this is also meaningless. It's just not . . . not important!

"Look, I don't know whether I'm explaining this right or not. It's not easy for me to put it into words. But something happened in that Indian hut that changed my life completely. It pushed away all the phoniness and all the lies that I'd been taught to believe were important for survival. Not body survival, screw that, but *soul* survival. Look," and she clutched my arm, "you write books about this kind of stuff. You know what I mean, don't you?"

Her voice was almost pleading. She so wanted someone else to understand what had happened to her—inside.

"Yes," I said. "I know what you mean."

"Thanks," she whispered and squeezed my hand.

# 13.
# The
# Spiritualistic
# Alliance

The religious belief known as Spiritualism has come a long way since the Fox Sisters heard those rappings in their New York State home back in 1848. It took hold in every country in the world and had millions of followers. In decline today, mostly because the various leaders refuse to bring their dogma up to date, it is still a vital force in Mexico.

It wasn't always that way, however. Spirits, ghosts, apparitions were familiar to Mexico, but interested individuals grouping together to study the messages received from spirits was a new tack. It was considered a novel and daring idea to hold sessions in private homes, to publish the findings, and to label these investigations a "religion."

Any religion that is not Catholicism has always had a tough time in Mexico. This new one, where the voices of long-departed Aunt Louisa and Uncle Rudolfo set the rules, was not to be tolerated by the Church or many of the political leaders. Not that the important people of the times didn't *believe* that Louisa and Rudolfo could come back from the grave, but why should they return and endorse a *new* religion when they had been Catholic in their mortal lives? If Spiritualism had remained a group affair like the Masons or the Rotary, the criticism wouldn't have been as severe, but by making itself a religion, it was asking for trouble.

These private home sessions began in 1861 in Guadalajara and went public for the first time in Mexico in 1868. In December of that year, Benigno Sanchez published the first issue of a Spiritualist magazine he called *La Ilustración Espírita.* It was a copy of a magazine called *La Revue Espirite* first published in 1858 by the Allan Kardek people in Paris.

Kardek was the pseudonym of a French doctor who decided to investigate, on a scientific basis, the messages and knocking coming from a popular household pastime called "table rapping." The facts that he and his assistants eventually compiled shook the man's educational and religious beliefs. *The Mediums Book*, his first published volume on the subject, was an instant best seller and eventually was translated into a dozen languages. A copy of it found its way to Brazil where Spiritualism quickly became a religion and was integrated with the other spirit beliefs. It is not surprising that Kardek's ideas next caught hold in Mexico even before they took hold in Spain.

Editor Sanchez' first issue had four pages and was crammed with translations of Kardek's doctrines and a plea for unity among the believers of Mexico. The publication caught on as fast as did the creed, and in the 1869 mid-year issue he wrote, "In 1861 there were no more than four or five adepts in Guadalajara. Now there are many hundreds in this city, multiplying daily on all social levels and causing serious desire to investigate on the part of those who just a short time ago looked at Spiritualism with a deprecating smile."

Such florid editorializing didn't stand in his way when it came to reporting, and in 1869 was published the first detailed account of a materialization session in Mexico. It was a historic psychic "first":

### SPIRIT WORKS

*We have already mentioned to our readers that there exists in this city an estimable lady who possesses the precious faculty of seeing the Spirits. Given an uncommonly high moral character and a complete abnegation to the truth, she is a delicate instrument who serves the Spirits to demonstrate their truths in such a way that only the ignorant and those of little faith could doubt.*

*Wednesday, the 21st of the current month, the following manifestations took place in the presence of more than 12 persons, some believers and others anxious to discover the truth.*

*Next to Sr. L. . . . . appeared a young woman of 22 years named Margarita, tall, regular complexion, and black hair. She had been dead for 17 years. She placed a star in front of him and told him:*

*"This star shall serve to light your path. Your light will not fall into darkness. Oh my friend! I will always be at your side guiding you and caring for your future. I am your guardian angel. Think on me."*

*She embraced him and departed. Sr. L. . . . . recognized her.*

*Afterward a spirit presented himself but did not give his name. He directed his words to the entire circle saying:*

*"Friends, we are united here to carry out investigations about a science that at present is not well known in our country. It will be of great value in combating the worries of those who feel that they will fall into an abyss after life is over. If we continue with these investigations, we will soon see our interest being repaid with great dividends. All sciences have had difficulties in the beginning and ours is no exception."*

*Then near Sr. F. . . . . there appeared the Spirit of an*

old man, about 80 years old. His clothing was the color of bricks, his nose large, his hair long, and in his hand he held a cane. He said his name was Juan and he said the following words:

"You are doing well, continue in this way. When you have abandoned your mortal covering I will be there to meet you. I am happy." Sr. F. . . . . recognized him.

Near Srta. D. . . . . appeared a spirit of a young man about 17 years old, who would have been that age today had he lived, but he died 40 days after his birth. He gave his name and the following words:

"Child, you are not mistaken. Many times I have come to you and I wish to be with you, but I cannot make my presence visible nor communicate with ease. I hope to do this when the system of communication has been perfected." Srta. D. . . . . recognized him, and these words alleviated some of the doubts that this young lady declared she held.

Afterward appeared four spirits, Pablo, Eduardo, Victoria and Ignacia. None of them were recognized. Then appeared General M. . . . . who said:

"I have not progressed a great deal as yet, but I hope to soon be able to give you revelations of some importance."

"Why don't you do it today?" asked Sr. V. . . . .

"Because nobody has called me. There is someone here who needs me and the least he could do would be to call me! If you do not put your mind in relation to mine, how can you expect this proof of survival to become registered on your mind? I am well. I am happier than when I held a high position among you, because I do not need to fight to keep it. Believe that I still live. If I am invisible for others, this does not mean that I have ceased living. In the universe everything is life and life here is of greater importance than on earth. How many sacrifices one must make as a man and how little is gained after so much suffering! In your world my path was not straight because I, like so many others, was under various influences, but the little bit of good that I did while I was among you has been a *recompense for me here. In a little while I will communicate with greater ease, for I still find it difficult to make you understand. Goodbye."* He was recognized *by several in the room.*

*Afterward appeared the spirit of a young man about 19 years old, regular height, thick features, eyes black and rapidly moving. He declared that 10 years ago he had left this city and had died of the fever about 6 or 7 years ago. It was a consequence of his dissipated life. He gave the first letters of his name, M and A.*

*He was* recognized *as the brother of one of those present.*

*Near Sr. E. . . . . appeared two spirits, Jorge and Angel. The first was father of the second. Sr. E. . . . .* recognized *them.*

*Of the 12 spirits who appeared, 7 were* recognized.

Committing suicide has always been one of the no-no's of Spiritualism, and in Mexico City in 1871 a medium went into trance and was contacted by a young man who had managed, after three attempts, to do himself in. The medium began to sweat and twist and cry out in pain as the spirit came lucidly—and agonizingly—through her:

*"This fire that is burning my eyes, my head, my brains. I feel the heat in the marrow of my bones . . . and this damned white light illuminates all my past actions . . . oh! . . . horrible! It makes me see all my past life, all my black thoughts, how horrible they are! I scream . . . I'm sorry . . . Oh damn! I will come near you and I will burn you all! Oh damn you! I hate you! Water! I need water! If I only had one drop . . . one single drop of water! I'm thirsty! Damn you, I need water! I need compassion! Nobody deserves it more than I do! . . . I demand it of you! . . I beseech you! . . . I pray you . . ."*

*At this the group around the medium began to pray for the poor tormented soul. Afterward came the following:*

*"Thank you. I've drunk the water that you have given me. Thank you and* ad—"

Commented the editor, "As you can see, his spirit could not express the word *'Dios'* [God] in order to leave us with the word *'adios'* [goodbye]."

*La Ilustración Espírita* folded after one year, but reappeared in the city of Guanajuato in 1870 with the same name and a new editor. This revamped and enlarged publication also lasted just one year. It was then in 1872 that General Refugio Gonzalez bought the name and the subscriber list and moved the publishing enterprise to Mexico City. He put a green paper cover on the magazine and filled it with engravings and line drawings showing the Spiritualist movement in all its aspects. In 1875 he founded the Spiritualist Society in Mexico City and became, through his publishing zeal, an honorary member of Spiritualist societies in such diverse places as Guatemala, Argentina, and France. He was well known in Mexican society and was a familiar figure with his war medals and his walking stick. More than once that stick was raised against editors of other newspapers who dared poke fun at his religion, against the ruffians who threw stones at his newspaper office windows, and at Catholic priests who denounced both the General and Spiritualism from their pulpits.

It is rumored that he once told a Cardinal to go to hell. It is a fact that in the twenty years that he published his magazine, he regularly supplied mediums and healers to the men who occupied the presidential palace. The crusty old General died in 1892 and his son, Moises, promised in a fiery editorial to carry on his father's mission. But enthusiasm has a way of deflating after a leader had gone, and the last issue of the magazine was dated December 1893. Other publications came and went over the next fifty years, but none of them had the impact of *La Ilustración Espírita.* Spiritualism itself went into a decline after the turn of the century and is today but a shadow of its former self. Groups still meet and small newspapers are still circulated, but the heyday was in the 1800s. Those days are past.

Every president of Mexico from the most honorably elected to the most cruel revolutionary have piously mouthed that they were devout Catholics and sons of the Church of Rome. All but one. He was Francisco Madero and he was a Spiritualist. More than that, he was a practicing medium who guided his life—and the future of his country—by the messages that came through his pen from his spirit guides Raul and José. Raul, strangely enough, was the spirit of his brother who died when the future president was only fourteen years old.

Francisco Madero was the son of a well-to-do rancher in Coahuila State. An avid reader but an agnostic and nonchurchgoer (much to his mother's consternation), Francisco was sent to Paris for his formal education and at age sixteen was introduced to the writings and meetings of the Kardek Spiritualists. This seemed to be exactly what he had been searching for.

When he returned to Mexico he brought back several of Kardek's books and a subscription to *La Revue Espirite* for his father, who was not impressed with the goings-on of the "other world." His father's world was his ranch and the management of several businesses in the area. He expected Francisco to have learned enough from his stay in Europe to handle these affairs and to make the businesses profitable. Francisco went to work for his father, gave up his outward interests in the spirits, but became a vegeterian because "they" had told him to do so.

Once the businesses were on solid footing, young Francisco began to reread the books and the newspapers he had brought with him. One night he received a strong mental impression to take a pen and paper and to sit quietly and wait for the message that was to appear. It was from his brother Raul, and it so convinced the young man that he determined never again to let the material world take precedence over that of the spirit. In his papers, which have been preserved in the National History Museum, Madero wrote of these automatic writing sessions:

"I soon developed the faculty where I could write with great facility. The communications that I received dealt with philosophical and moral questions and were in a language so beautiful that not only was I surprised but those who read them and knew of my poor command of the Spanish language as well. These communications led me to understand the basis of spiritual philosophy, above all the most moral parts of it. The spirits soon transformed me from a young useless libertine into a man of justice who was concerned about the welfare of the country and who had to serve Mexico with all my strength." His writings had told him: "Francisco, one day you will be President of Mexico."

During most of Madero's young life, Mexico had been ruled by a tyrant named Porfirio Díaz. The man had the backing of the army, the wealthy, and the Church. He also had the backing of the United States Government. Free elections and free speech had long become a thing of the past. Madero saw Díaz as Mexico's true enemy, and consulted with the spirits as to how to bring about his downfall. The spirits guided him all the way.

By 1910, Madero was the greatest mediator and strategist in the country, and men like Pancho Villa and Emiliano Zapata listened to him and planned their revolutionary tactics accordingly. His genius united most of Mexico in its battle against Díaz, and in the spring of 1911 the tyrant's thirty-year stranglehold on Mexico came to an end. He was sent to exile in France.

Madero refused to accept the presidency, insisting instead that the revolutionary leaders choose a provisional president and hold free elections. When he came to the capital, crowds flocked to see him, blocking his way with flowers and wild cheering. But as he was giving his speech, a tremendous earthquake hit Mexico City. Walls tumbled, buildings shook, great fissures opened in the earth and swallowed people. The ancient church of Santo Domingo was wrecked. An army barracks collapsed, killing thirty-three soldiers. A great crack appeared in the walls of the presidential palace, displacing the keystone of the arch which Díaz had passed daily during his thirty-year reign. The quake lasted fourteen minutes and 207 people died. To the superstitious it meant that the gods were angry that they had forced Días out of office and they began to look with frightened eyes at Madero and his spirit guides.

Madero managed to win the election in spite of this omen, mainly because there were so many other candidates who divided the ballot. His wasn't a large majority, but it was the winning majority.

While the spirits had guided him to the presidential chair, they weren't very careful in the men they chose to be around him and weren't very wise about the unrest that was still seething in the interior. They also were completely in the dark about the unhappiness the United States felt at seeing Madero president, and they did nothing to thwart the plans and underhanded C.I.A.-like dealings of United States Ambassador Henry Wilson. President Taft was sure Madero would take over all American investments and ordered several thousand troops poised at the border ready to fight. The Mexican generals began squabbling among themselves and often destroyed entire towns in their pocket civil wars. Finally Pancho Villa and Zapata came back into the fight and Madero, after several disastrous political decisions, was arrested and imprisoned in Mexico City. On Washington's birthday, 1913, shots rang out from the prison yard where Madero was held. He had tried to escape, the guards reported, and they had shot him. The term of office, the spirits had promised him lasted less than two years. The bloodshed in the revolution-torn country would last another seven.

A strange story that the Spiritualists loved but the other Mexicans shuddered at took place in Mexico City in 1953. It leaked out to the press because the professor was so shaken by the incident that he told his high-school class about it and they, of course, immediately told their families and friends.

Upon leaving his school one evening, Professor Roberto Seabra was met by a man in a chauffeur's uniform. He was the driver of Sra. Carmen Portillo Zaragoza, and she was quite ill. Could the professor please come at once and visit her? The limousine was waiting.

Sra. Zaragoza was an old friend of the professor's, but he hadn't seen her in quite a while. He had heard that the lady had been traveling overseas, and his school work had kept him quite busy. He now tried to find out exactly what was wrong with the woman, but the driver was tight-lipped and said very little on the way over. When they arrived at the mansion, the professor noted with just a twinge of envy that the house and gardens were still the most beautiful he had ever seen. The driver led the way up the curving staircase to the lady's bedroom.

"I was surprised to see her looking so thin and pale. Beside the bed was a small table with various medicine bottles and a pitcher of water. She explained that she had asked me to come because she was sure she was going to die, and there were certain personal matters that she wanted me to handle for her. Of course I protested that she looked fine and wasn't to think about such a thing. I even suggested that she call a doctor."

"No, professor," the lady replied. "I don't want to see any more doctors or take any more of their medicines. I'm sick of doctors! I would rather die. That's why I am asking you to do these things for me."

She gave the professor a list of items to be dealt with in case of her death. When he insisted that she take some of the medicines on the table, he was able to get a teaspoon of some yellow liquid down her throat. She laughed and said it would have tasted better with muscatel wine for a chaser. Around midnight he let himself out the front door and took a taxi back to his apartment.

The next day he awoke early and went to see a friend of his who was a medical doctor. He begged the man to

come and see Sra. Zaragoza, but much to his frustration
the doctor told him to sit quietly and have a cigarette. The
doctor suggested that possibly the professor needed a vacation—he knew the medical history of Sra. Zaragoza, and
there wasn't anything he could do.

Furious with his friend's attitude, the professor left the
doctor's office and took a taxi to her home. Much to his
surprise, the garden that had looked so lovely in the moon-
light was now overgrown and weed-filled. The house was
shuttered and the paint peeling from the front door. When
he tried the bell and didn't hear it ring, he began to pound
on the door with his fists. There was no answer. He
became more and more desperate over his friend's safety
and began banging on the door with a rock.

This brought the gardener of the neighboring house to
see what all the noise was about. "There is nobody home,
señor," the man said.

"But how could they have left the lady alone?" asked
the professor. "She is too ill to be left alone and too weak
to travel."

"What lady?" asked the gardener.

"Why Sra. Zaragoza, of course!"

"Oh, señor. Then you don't know? Sra. Zaragoza is
dead."

"What do you mean, dead?" shouted the professor. "I
was with her only last night! That's a very unfunny joke!"
and he continued to pound on the door.

Soon a small crowd had gathered, watching him
curiously. Finally a policeman appeared and grabbed his
hand.

"I must get in to see Sra. Zaragoza," the professor
shouted to him. "It's a matter of life and death."

"It is only a matter of death, señor," replied the
officer. "Sra. Zaragoza has been dead for eight months.
For eight months this house has been closed. Now I sug-
gest that you go about your business, or I will have to take
you into headquarters."

The professor returned to his classroom. He told the

story to his students. "Do you think this really happened," he asked them, "or do you think I'm going crazy?"

In the mid-1940s, a middle-aged man with a crippled leg became one of Mexico City's best known mediums. His name is Luisito. He had been "surrounded by spirits" all his young life. This hadn't helped him any as he grew up because as an orphan going from family to family, he should not have frightened the very people who wanted to help him. He married and came to Mexico City to take any position he could handle with his one bad leg. He managed to get a job at the national pawn shop known as Monte de Piedade. There he discovered that his supervisor was a Spiritualist minister, and soon he was attending development sessions and progressing faster than anyone in the group.

His speciality was materializations. Those who have seen him, say he was able to produce several clearly-defined figures at each session. These figures often permitted themselves to be touched and examined and would carry on conversations with their friends and family. The top psychic investigators in Mexico of his day examined Luisito, yet under rigid conditions he produced his ghostly phenomena time after time. (A materialization in his case was the formation of a human figure from a substance called ectoplasm that came from his body as he was in trance. Sometimes the white smoky substance could be seen coming from his mouth, his nose, his eyes, and his solar plexus. Many mediums were supposedly able to do this in the early days of Spiritualism, but it is now, along with seances and floating trumpets, becoming a lost metaphysical art.)

One of Luisito's most important clients was Mexican President Miguel Aleman. The medium was called to the presidential palace at least once a week, if not more frequently, to contact the spirits of great statesmen who had governed Mexico and other countries in order to aid Aleman in coming to the right decisions for his country. Because of this patronage, Luisito built up a clientele during the 40s and 50s that included just about every important name in Mexico.

One of his biggest fans and closest friends now is Sra. Evangelina Padilla de Lelo de Larrea. Her father was once Vice President of Mexico and an unsuccessful presidential candidate who often had Luisito to his home for materialization sessions. In her sumptuous home in the Colonia Lomas Virreyes, Doña Evangelina told me about Luisito and what she had seen with her own eyes. With her was her socially prominent friend María Teresa Bertotto Amezcua of Cuernavaca. Doña Evangelina looks after Luisito now that he is approaching eighty and refuses to see anyone at all. Cataracts on both eyes and his crippled leg have turned him into a recluse. He no longer uses his power. It's not necessary to bring back the spirits to make a living. His three grown children now support him.

"In 1957 there was a materialization session right here in this house," Doña Evangelina told me. "I purposely made sure that all the doors and windows were closed and locked and that there was no way any outsider could get into this living room. There were eight people here that night, and they all saw the same thing I did.

"We had prepared a pot of warm wax and put it on a side table. Luisito sat in a chair and we tied his arms and legs. Then he went into trance. We turned off the lights and waited. Then slowly the white smoke came from his body and formed the physical body of his teacher Mahur. We asked Mahur to put his hand into the warm wax because we wanted physical proof that he had been there. The spirit traveled across the table and over to the other side table where the pot was sitting. It was easily twelve feet away from where Luisito was sitting. The figure crossed *through* the table where we were sitting and plunged his hand into the wax. It stayed there for about five minutes. Then it vanished. We put on the lights and sure enough, the form where the hand had been was impressed into the wax. We've made plaster casts of it and I've kept one for myself." She pointed to a clenched hand that was sitting on the coffee table in front of me.

"Another time, at a session with fifteen people present, Luisito went into trance. After the lights were turned off a figure began to materialize in the center of the room. Luisito was sitting, tied to his chair, in a corner. First we saw the feet, then the legs and body, then the arms and hands. Finally the face appeared. The apparition walked around the room and let each of us touch him. He was solid but cold. I felt the texture of his clothing and the smoothness of his skin, but there was no warmth. Then he walked over to one woman who had been complaining of migraine headaches and he touched her. Her headache went away and, as far as I know, never came back. Another woman in the group suffered from arthritis pains in her hips. After this apparition touched her, she never had another pain."

"That's very unusual," I said. "In all my research I've never heard of a materialization form curing anyone."

"It didn't happen often," she replied, "but when a healing was needed, one was given."

"I'll admit I was a doubter," her friend Sra. Bertotto spoke up. "I had gone to one of Luisito's sessions and while I was impressed, I couldn't believe it was true. Then I went to a second session. All the lights were turned off and Luisito was in trance and tied to his chair, when some-one made the mistake of opening the door from the out-side and letting in some light. It was just enough time and light to let me see that everyone was still in his original place and that Luisito was still asleep in his chair. The only other person there was this white figure walking around in the middle of the room and touching people. There was the figure, and there was Luisito. That did it. From then on I was convinced."

"The light didn't bother the figure?" I asked. I had heard the story of a materialization medium in the United States who was doing a stage demonstration in front of a large audience. Even though he had asked everyone present not to turn on any lights, not even to light a match, one woman stood up and took a flash picture of an apparition. Immediately the figure vanished, and the shock to the medium's nervous system kept him in the intensive care ward of the local hospital for over a week.

"No, the light didn't seem to bother either Luisito or the apparition. But it helped me a great deal. I'm a practicing Catholic, and it was very important proof to me that this was all real."

At another session this same lady took her sister, who was an even greater scoffer than she herself had been. "My sister thought all this was pure nonsense and consented to go with me only because she wanted to show me how foolish I had been behaving. I think she felt that if she proved Luisito to be a fake, I would escape seven years in Purgatory or something like that. Well, the medium went into trance and the lights went out. Soon a single hand appeared in the center of the room and floated up toward the ceiling. Everything was in silence, but my sister broke it by whispering in a loud voice: 'Oh come on! That's being done with smoke and a movie projector!' Well, the hand paused, then came streaking down toward my sister. The next thing we heard was a loud smack on my sister's head and then she howled in pain. There was laughter in the darkness *across* the room."

Doña Evangelina showed me two objects that had materialized for her during Luisito's sessions. One was a music box that plays "Rock A Bye Baby," and the other was a silver cup with the profile of a woman's face clearly etched in the bottom.

She tells of the session where a spirit appeared and gave them communion. "It was the form of a priest whom the entire family had known when he was alive. He put the Host in our mouths and we could taste it and feel it when we swallowed."

Luisito always asked that The Lord's Prayer be said before he began his sessions. At times, only a hand or a face would materialize, or Luisito's own hands and face would glow with a white light. Once four beings appeared at the same time and answered questions as they moved around the room. It was this moving that impressed people, for these figures moved rapidly. Luisito, with his painfully crippled leg, moved slowly. With that bad leg, there was no way he could have done the physical phenomena himself.

Doña Evangelina's most emotional session came three months after her mother died. "I hadn't asked Luisito for this, because as a good Catholic I didn't want to disturb my mother's soul. But slowly there she was, materializing in front of me in the middle of the darkened room. Her entire body appeared. She didn't say anything. She just came over to me and began to stroke my hair. When she was alive she like to touch my hair. It was my mother's touch. There was no doubting it. Naturally, I was quite moved by this, and I cried."

It has been estimated that well over five hundred people have seen these manifestations of Luisito's—not only willing believers like Doña Evangelina and her friends but parapsychologists, medical doctors, reporters, writers and scientists. Some scientifically minded organizations in Mexico City attempt to look into the unusual talents of people like Luisito, but they are few and their personnel unqualified.

Cuauhtémoc is a national hero in Mexico. He was the successor to Moctezuma and died rather than give in to Cortez and his invaders. Now Cuauhtémoc has returned to life—in spirit form—to inhabit the body of a frail, publicity-shy woman healer known as Pachita.

I tried to see Pachita when I was researching this book, but a handful of "guards and friends" decided to keep me away. They spoke of spirituality and the need to tell the world about the powers of spirit, yet even though I did manage to get her on the phone one afternoon and hear her tell me she would see me at my convenience, they blocked all my efforts so successfully that I never got close to the woman. Her guards never let me through.

Pachita's fame had traveled as far as the United States. When I told a parapsychologist in New York that I was planning a trip to Mexico, he told me to be sure to interview Pachita. He had met a man who supposedly had been born deaf and had been healed with just one visit to Pachita. She had taken a knife, jabbed it in his ear and twisted it. When she removed it, his hearing was restored.

In Mexico City I met a university professor who said he had witnessed several of Pachita's operations. The most impressive one was with a man who needed open heart surgery. He claims that Pachita opened the man's chest with a large knife. The man was lying there with no anesthesia of any kind, and while Pachita sliced at the heart with a small paring knife, he held the heart in his hands so she could get a better angle on it. And this from a university professor!

*Claudia,* the top woman's magazine in Mexico, did four pages on Pachita, but were unable to interview her personally or even get a snapshot of her. In their article they claim she restored the voice of a popular singer, removed the cataracts from a woman's eyes in a few minutes, and took out the kidneys of a male patient, washed them free of stones, and replaced them. They even ran a pro-and-con article about the healer. The negative side was taken by a Mexican medical doctor who admitted that Pachita was "working at different mental levels when she was in trance." The pro side was written by an ex-president of the Institute of Parapsychological Studies in Mexico who said he had witnessed several of Pachita's operations, "and I held a knife as she pushed it into the stomach of a patient. It is incredible the way she operates without ... anesthetics and without the patient feeling any pain or unpleasant aftereffects."

Pachita was born, illegitimately, somewhere around 1915. Her first healing came when she was a girl of nine visiting a traveling circus that had set up tents in a small interior town. The female elephant was having great difficulty in giving birth to her calf and the local veterinarians and medical doctors could not help her. It was thought that in order to save the baby they would have to kill the mother. Pachita, as the story goes, suddenly went into trance and with all the bearing of an Aztec emperor, began giving orders as to how the calf should be handled. The startled circus owners obeyed the ragged little girl and the baby elephant was delivered.

Sometime after that, Pachita was taken into a Catholic convent and trained as a nun, but her healings of both animals and humans (slashing them with knives while speaking with a deep voice) so upset the Sisters that they forced her to leave, positive she was working with the Devil.

Pachita lives in a small house in a nondescript area of Mexico City guarded by ten enormous, frequently defecating dogs and her group of advisors. In the past few years, she has not had an easy time of it. More than once she has been arrested for practicing medicine without a license, and rumor has it she was often beaten in her cell by policemen who wanted some of her supposed wealth. It's also said that one time the governor of a northern state personally got her out of jail.

I have heard, too, that she has lost her powers, that Cuauhtémoc's visits are now few and far between, and that is why she has stopped seeing strangers and has even dropped her old friends and assistants and permitted herself to be protected by this band of "guards."

Mexican parapsychologist Dr. Carlos Ortiz de la Huerta defends Pachita and gets upset when he thinks of the way his people have treated her. "Pachita is an extraordinary woman, a very good woman. It seems that we are still in the time of the Inquisition. We persecute these healers with a vengeance in spite of the good they have done. They are hated if they succeed or if they fail. They are feared for their paranormal powers and equated with the Devil. What irritates parapsychologists," he says, "is that the public refuses to accept that there is another reality aside from the one we are living in and that it can be reached only through the application of extrasensory faculties."

# 14.
# Mary King, The Sanctuary, and El Templo de la Fe

It is rather surprising that the top medium in Mexico should be blonde, speak perfect English, and have a name like Mary King, but that's how it is. She is Mexican, born in Mexico and her Mexican family tree goes back four generations.

Yet she remains terribly British, with her close-cropped yellow hair, her small features, and Buckingham Palace accent. Her command of Spanish is flawless and she can switch from one language to the other with lightning speed. Often, in an animated conversation, she'll move in and out of both languages, quite unaware that she's doing it.

Her prestige in Spiritualist circles all over the world is impressive, yet she remains shy, unassuming and at times, doubts that she has any abilities whatsoever. She would rather talk about her father's abilities, and getting her to talk about herself is like pulling teeth. In fact, it took me several personal visits and several social functions together before she would consent to an interview at all. She has a slight tremor to her voice. Her delicate hands flutter like small birds even when she tries to still them in her lap. Her eyes are a bright yet soft shade of blue, and the few lines that have begun to form around them are the only clues that she is on the other side of forty.

"I have many stories I could tell you," she said with a nervous smile, "but one of my favorites is the one I tell psychiatrists. They never want to believe it." She laughs, slightly embarrassed that she is about to talk about herself. "I was at a tea party here in Mexico City and sitting and chatting with two friends of mine when I became aware of a man in spirit. He was standing in front of me and trying to catch my attention. Then he spoke. 'I am Alex,' he said, 'and I want to talk to you. I am Alex.'

"So I turned to the two women beside me. I knew one of them was interested in Spiritualism, and I said as calmly as I could, 'Do either of you know an Alex who has passed into the world of spirit?'

"One lady said, 'Yes, an Alex Popovitch.'

"I looked at the spirit, and he smiled and said, 'Yes, that's me.' Then he said, 'You must give a message to my wife.'

"Well, I told him that I didn't know his wife and certainly I couldn't call her up out of the blue. I told him I needed proof that he was really who he said he was. I'll admit, David, that I was beginning to wonder if I wasn't going a little bit nuts. I mean there I was at a proper afternoon tea party balancing a cup and saucer on my lap and asking a ghost to prove he wasn't telling me a lie.

"Anyway, he showed me a large gold cross at the end of a thick chain. 'Tell my wife about this and she'll know that I am real,' he said. I told him that that wouldn't do at all, that everybody in Mexico had a cross and chain. He would have to give me something else. 'But only my wife and I know about *this* cross,' he insisted. I insisted right back that it wasn't proof enough. So then he showed me an icon, one of those Russian religious pieces, that had the Virgin Mary painted on it. It was just the Virgin by herself, she didn't hold a child. 'Tell my wife about the cross and describe this icon," he said to me. 'That will be proof enough.'

" 'Well, suppose I do,' I told him. 'What good do you expect to come from it?'

" 'I am very worried about my wife,' he said. 'Ever since I died she won't go out, she won't leave the house. If she keeps this up, she is going to become psychologically very ill. Christmas is coming, and I want her to get back into the world. I want her to accept the invitations that are coming for her. I want her to lead a normal life. Please tell her that I'm very happy over here and that I want to help her, but I can't help her if she stays at home and becomes a recluse. I can't cut through her grief. I've tried.' Then he disappeared.

"So I asked the lady beside me if she would phone Mrs. Popovitch and ask her to call me. I'm afraid I was too chicken to call her directly. Two days later Marie Popovitch rang me up. I told her exactly what had happened at the tea party. Once she got over her surprise she said that yes, it was true, Alex always kept an icon beside his bed and it was only the Virgin and not the Christ child as well. The night Alex died she slipped a large golden cross on a thick chain into his coffin. No-one saw her do it. Only she and Alex knew she would do it.

"Later she called to tell me that what impressed her even more than my message was that soon after I had talked to her, her telephone rang. One call was asking her for dinner on Christmas Eve and another call was inviting her for Christmas dinner. 'I remembered your message,' she said, 'and I accepted both invitations.' She sent me a little cross as a thank-you gift.

"I like this story," Mary said, "because I didn't know the lady at all. I had never met her or her husband, and I certainly didn't know about the cross or the icon. Even the woman at the tea party didn't know about the cross and the icon. I feel this is a good story for psychiatrists and all the other doubters because it proves that I wasn't 'reading' *anybody's* mind. As far as I'm concerned, it is absolute proof of survival after death."

Mary King comes by her talents naturally, for her father Kenneth Bannister was internationally known for his work in Mexican Spiritualist circles. In fact, he built a psychic center that became the most important Sanctuary in all Mexico.

Kenneth Bannister didn't start out as a spiritual man. When he wasn't even fifteen, he began his career as a soldier in the British Army by lying about his age and being sent off to Gallipoli. There he saw action and death at first hand. He was with the Army when it took Jerusalem, and he was on a first-name basis with Lawrence of Arabia. After so much time on a horse, he became interested in a new gadget called a flying machine and was one of the first to join the Royal Flying Corps and become a pilot. When the First World War was over, he still itched for excitement and decided to go to Brazil and hunt for gold in the Amazon. But a Mexican friend who had been stranded in England during the war convinced him to stop off in Mexico instead. There would be no problem, he was told, in getting a well-paid position as a flying instructor with the Mexican Army. But when he arrived in Mexico he found airplanes were almost unknown and the government didn't have an air force. Penniless, he took a job piloting a Mexico City streetcar instead.

His mother had always been interested in Spiritualism and regularly sent him bundles of Spiritualist newspapers and magazines which he tossed away. But now that he didn't have extra money to buy books of his own, he began to read these publications. It wasn't long before he became a dedicated Spiritualist himself. Using the precepts found in that literature, he began to call upon spirits for guidance and soon was offered an unexpected job with a newly established English firm called the Portland Cement Manufacturing Company. They needed a shift boss at their plant who could speak both English and Spanish.

With money in his pocket for the first time in many years, he began to seriously court an attractive young lady who was born in Mexico but had English ancestors. Her grandparents had settled in Mexico in the 1860s; another side of her family had been French and had accompanied the Emperor Maximillian on his ill-fated attempt to turn Mexico into a European-style monarchy. This man, Colonel Reynault, was also psychic advisor to the Emperor and his wife. One wonders if he saw, and reported, the obvious handwriting on the wall.

Madys Hamer was psychic herself, and so were her brothers and her mother and father. They had been holding seances and spirit development circles for years, and young Kenneth Bannister fitted into the family perfectly. Notes had been kept of messages that had come through her brother William who acted as the medium for the circles during the war, and almost everything that was predicted through him came to pass.

Using his Spiritualist beliefs (he was positive his father was guiding him), Kenneth Bannister moved up into the company. When a new plant was built at Tolteca, he was promoted to its manager. By this time he and Madys had four children, Kenneth Jr., Mary, Peter, and Miriam.

"My father always knew he was protected," Mary remembers, "because we all went through some terrible times and he was never harmed. There were times when he would have to fire a workman and the man would vow to kill him for it. One man threatened to shoot my father on sight, yet my father refused to carry a gun. I can remember being put into the cellar when bandits rode through the factory grounds shooting at everyone and trying to loot as much as they could. Once we children and my mother were walking down a road when we came to a man who had been hanged from a telegraph pole. Groups used to take justice into their own hands and they had strung this man up and left him there for everyone to see. I remember how my mother turned us around and brought us home. She tried to tell us stories to erase the memory of that man from our eyes, but it was impossible.

"Because I was the manager's daughter, it was very difficult to find other children who were allowed to play with me. So when strange little children came and played with me, I was delighted. I told my mother about them and she thought it was perfectly normal, but one day when I realized that my older brother couldn't see them, I became frightened. They went away and never came back.

"My brother Peter died when he was quite young, and soon he began coming back to play with me in spirit as we had played together on this level. This didn't frighten me. My mother sensed his presence and knew when he was in the house. It was quite natural that he should do this, and none of us thought anything about it. Even though he died when he was small, he actually grew up with us. He has never stopped appearing to me, and he's become my guide. When I have to do any contacting on the other side, it is Peter who brings the spirit over to me. I always go to him for advice when I have a problem that I can't seem to solve on my own. When we would have the home circles, he would often come through in direct voice. He's grown up now and is quite a handsome young man. His main work over there seems to be that of helping young people adjust to their new life in spirit.

"Then we moved back to Mexico City when my father was made general manager of the company. My mother thought things would be easier for us then, but at the time of President Cárdenas when the government expropriated the oil companies, there was violence and strikes at the cement factories as well. I remember one incident when the workers had seized the plant and locked in everyone who had been in the offices. They put up barricades and refused to let anyone bring food to the prisoners. Even though they all had guns, my father walked through the lines and took food to his employees. He was never harmed. He said he asked for spirit protection and knew he received it. He was completely fearless because he knew nothing could happen to him.

"One day my father took the streetcar and came out to San Angel. Today it is an expensive, developed part of Mexico City, but in the late thirties it was considered an isolated, rural area. People would go there for vacations, but never considered living there and working in the city. He got up on a rooftop and looked down into an enormous garden with one house at its edge. He knew immediately that this was to be his home. He searched and found the owner and after months of bargaining back and forth, managed to buy the place. When we moved out here my mother's relatives all cried. They thought we were moving so far away that none of them would ever see us again.

"My father took the house and redesigned it. He didn't have a formal education, he'd never graduated from any schools, but he had this innate knowledge about architecture and interior design. He also knew a great deal about interior decorating. In fact, a book was published in America about the most beautiful homes in the world, and my father's house was included in it. He loved to garden and he planned the enormous space himself. He planted trees, built a reflectory pool and several bird sanctuaries. It was funny how birds loved him. Every morning he would go out into the garden just after sunrise, and there would be hundreds of birds waiting silently for him. As soon as they saw him they would begin to sing and come around him for food. He never kept a bird in a cage, yet the wild birds of Mexico became quite tame for him. They seemed to know he was their friend."

Kenneth Bannister was eventually made president of Portland Cement in Mexico even though his outspoken views on Spiritualism (while working for a Protestant corporation in a Catholic country) created controversy wherever he went. It wasn't as "fashionable" in those days to admit a belief in spirits and psychic phenomena as it is today, yet he never backed down or apologized for his beliefs. "As children we used to get embarrassed when he would argue for Spiritualism with important people," his daughter recalls. "More than one person walked away from him at London cocktail parties because he refused to let them poke fun at his religion. That's why we were very pleased when Queen Elizabeth decorated him and gave him the C.D.E., because many people thought that an honor from the government would not come to a man who was so outspokenly a Spiritualist."

Kenneth Bannister didn't get this highest honor because of his beliefs, but because the Mexican government had told the British government what a fine job he had done for relations between the two countries. When he retired from the company, the Mexican newspapers ran articles praising him as "the ideal example of how a foreigner could work among us and help Mexico to grow."

Kenneth's wife Madys was a medium in her own right, but she never practiced it professionally and was afraid of going into trance. "She used her abilities in her daily life," Mary recalls "and we grew to depend on those gifts for constant guidance. Right after the Second World War, my brother Kenneth was to be discharged from the Canadian Army. But then we got a letter from him saying it would be at least two years before they would let him out because the Army didn't want to get rid of everyone at once. He was sorry that he wouldn't be able to spend Christmas with us. My father had gone to London on one of the first commercial flights from Mexico after the war and had promised that he'd be home in time for Christmas. My mother had other ideas. 'My husband Kenneth won't be back for Christmas, but my *son* Kenneth will be,' she predicted.

"We knew enough not to question her. One morning she came into my bedroom and told me to awaken the chauffeur because Kenneth Jr. was arriving on the eleven o'clock train from the United States. 'Did he telephone or send a telegram?' I asked. No, he hadn't done any of those things, my mother just knew he would be at the station at eleven.

"I awoke the driver and we all went to the railroad station. The man at the information counter said there wasn't any eleven o'clock train, but that the train from the States was very late for some reason. At five minutes to eleven that train pulled in and my brother Kenneth got off of it. He told us his discharge papers had come so suddenly he didn't have time even for a phone call before he caught the train. He wasn't at all surprised to see my mother at the station. He just took it for granted. I guess I did too, because I had gotten out of bed and awakened the driver. And yes, my father had to stay on in England because of an unexpected business problem and didn't get home for Christmas after all."

When Mary married, Mr. Bannister built her a large Spanish-style home at one corner of the garden, and built his daughter Miriam a large house on another corner of the walled-in garden when she married. He had no further building plans until suddenly his wife became ill with a growth in her throat, was rushed to the hospital, was operated on and died. She had only been forty-eight years old.

For this man who had devoted himself entirely to his wife and family, it was a crushing blow. "My father just couldn't understand what he had done to have taken away from him the one thing he cared about so much. He felt my mother had been his soul mate. When she died, he vowed he would never marry again. He decided that from then on he would devote his life to helping others."

It was in his wife's memory that the construction of the fourth building in the garden was begun. It was to be a Sanctuary, a place where those in need could come for spiritual guidance and spiritual healing. It was to be a place of love and hope, a permanent memory to his beloved Madys. It is a beautifully designed, curved two-story red brick building with large windows and white shutters. The large trees that were untouched during the construction keep the walkways and the patio shaded and cool. Inside the floors are of polished red stones, and the whitewashed walls are crossed with dark wood beams that also support the ceilings. Mexican tiles decorate the insides of the downstairs rooms and the large fireplace. There are three bedrooms for visiting mediums and for healing and private sessions. A special blue color predominates these rooms. It was a color Madys chose when she spoke through a medium while the Sanctuary was being built.

He retired to give his full attention to the Sanctuary. Now wealthy from his position in the company and through shrewd investments through spirit guidance, he began to give his healing talents freely. He would work on as many as five hundred people a month and never charge them one centavo. Should they wish to leave a donation, he would accept it and later give the money to a needy person. On his death, Mary would find a list of forty people that he had been supporting for years.

He didn't like magnetic passes and didn't use herbs and amulets. He just placed his hands on the ill person and permitted the energy to flow through him. Mary recalls a child with a kidney disease whom the doctors had completely given up on. After four visits to the Sanctuary, the child was cured. Another man suffered from a nervous condition and had traveled all over the world to consult the best medical men about it. None of them could do a thing, yet he was cured with just one session with Kenneth Bannister. As his fame grew, the crowds of those needing help grew as well, and he invited other healers to come and work with him, paying those healers from his own pocket.

He set up lectures and development classes and while Mary worked there as a practicing medium, others came from the United States and Europe. Famed Los Angeles medium Brenda Crenshaw spent several weeks there, as did Maurice Barbanell the medium and editor of the London-based newspaper *Psychic News*. Arthur Ford, perhaps America's greatest psychic, was a frequent guest there. The list could go on for pages. Because most of the Sanctuary's clients were Mexican, the lectures and readings and private sessions were immediately translated into Spanish. Some very rich people came to the Sanctuary, but it was filled mostly with the very poor.

One British medium, John Lovette, stands out vividly in Mary's mind. He had come to Mexico to work with Mr. Bannister and hold development classes. One of his specialties was apports, material objects produced out of thin air. It was Mary's responsibility to prepare the seance room, to make it completely dark, and to be sure all doors, windows, and other openings were sealed and blocked.

"One afternoon John was to hold a session in the small private sanctuary on the roof of my father's house. It was actually the third floor of the building, a small room that my father and mother both loved. After I had prepared the room, John told me that he had invited a young man named Harold as his guest. But he warned me that Harold didn't believe any of this stuff and to be sure that Harold didn't try to touch him once he went into trance. To touch a medium in trance can sometimes be fatal. So when the session began I sat Harold down beside me where I could control him. But when John went into trance and a small white light began to float around the room, Harold was out of his chair trying to grab the light. I couldn't hold onto him and I silently asked my guide for help. Then a little girl's voice was heard coming out of the darkness. 'We are going to bring some flowers for Harold,' it said. 'Please tell Harold to sit in his chair, put his hands on his lap palms upward because we are bringing an apport especially for him.'

"I could feel Harold sit down beside me and then I felt something moving past my face. Harold groaned and said, 'This is very heavy!' He remained seated for the rest of the session. When the lights were turned on, there sat Harold with an enormous flower pot in his lap. It was one of the two-feet-wide ones that had been down in the patio. Filled with dirt, it weighed a couple hundred pounds. It took three men to lift it off Harold and carry it back down the three flights of stairs to the patio. It took three men, but spirit had raised it in an instant up three flights and through the walls of the locked room. The flowers in the pot died soon after, unfortunately, but it made a believer out of Harold, so I suppose it was worth it.

"One of the only real materializations that I ever saw was when John brought through a child at one of his sessions. I saw this mist forming at my feet and then watched as it swirled up like a small whirlwind and it became a child. It moved across the room and then went down into nothingness. I was quite impressed."

Kenneth Bannister was never condemned from any pulpit in Mexico for his "work with the Devil." He was open to receive anyone from any faith who was also open enough to listen to his side of the argument. He was known to be extremely honest in business, and this carried him over when his religious beliefs were questioned. The Mexicans figured that any man who was so honest and intelligent would not devote his life to trickery and charlatanism. Since he didn't charge money at the Sanctuary, he couldn't be accused of fleecing the poor. (He always thought that one of the biggest problems mediums faced was the need to support themselves through their gifts.) A gentle person who seldom raised his voice, he was successful in everything he did. "He was one of the few people I have met in my life," Mary recalls, "who lived his beliefs. He thought you had to help as many people as you possibly could in your lifetime. To him the most important thing was that you really loved people. I truly cannot remember him saying anything unkind about anybody."

Kenneth Bannister had a brain tumor that he kept under control with cortisone injections. He wasn't happy with it and hoped that it would take him quickly and with a minimum of pain. The one thing he did not want was to remain alive in a hospital like a wired-up vegetable. At the beginning of January, 1975, his headaches became more frequent but he continued his work. Mary noticed a flash of pain across his face from time to time, but when she inquired he refused to mention it.

On a Monday, his youngest daughter Miriam went to

see the medium Leslie Flint in London. To her surprise her mother came through. Madys said she had been waiting for Kenneth to come over for a long time. She wanted him with her, and his physical body would never be cured. "You have had him for a long time, and now it's my turn," the voice said. "He is about to pass over. Don't be saddened by this because if you knew how happy we were over here, none of you would worry about dying." Miriam, in London, not wanting to upset Mary in Mexico, didn't tell her of this message.

Three days later, Kenneth Bannister complained that the headaches were worse. When the doctor arrived he ordered an ambulance and told the dying man he was going to the hospital. "I don't want to be kept alive in a hospital," he told Mary as he was being taken from his home. Mary, stopping to grab some money and credentials, glanced up at a drawing of her father's spirit guide, Silver Birch. "The eyes of this drawing told me he was going to pass over."

On the way to the hospital, Kenneth Bannister died. Mary, riding in the back with him, insisted that the driver return home, but the driver had other orders. He would take the body to a funeral parlor. When they stopped at an emergency clinic for verification of the death, Mary jumped from the ambulance and sat on the curb. She refused to go to any funeral parlor. She refused to get back into the ambulance until the driver had promised to take her father's body back home. Fearing a struggle with a hysterical female, the driver turned the ambulance around and Kenneth Bannister came home.

"I think funerals are barbaric," Mary says, "and I wasn't going to let any stranger touch my father's body. Someone brought a coffin and some candles and I placed them in the Sanctuary. Then I wrapped my father's body in a blanket and put it in the coffin. I picked some flowers from the garden and put them in with him. Then I shut the lid.

"My guides had told me to stay by the coffin until daybreak, so I sat there by myself. It was very beautiful, for there were lights and flashes all over the room. I would see a flash of light and say, 'Is so-and-so here?' and the light would flash again. The strangest thing was that the coffin was enveloped in the most beautiful blue flames I've ever seen. They were very very strong and they lasted all night. A friend of mine told me that she saw these same flames at her husband's feet when he was dying. The candle flames never flickered once. They were absolutely still and I felt the room was filled with people. It was absolutely beautiful. I felt great happiness, and I kept saying to my father 'Isn't this wonderful?'

"About ten minutes to six I fell asleep and was awakened by this touch on my cheek. I looked up and saw my father looking very young. He was with my mother. They both smiled at me, and held hands and walked out of the Sanctuary and into the garden. I looked out of the window, and it was dawn. Suddenly all the birds began to sing as one. A friend of mine who had arrived to console me said, 'Isn't it funny that there was one moment when all the birds started singing?' Then suddenly I felt the room was empty. I was left with the flowers and the candles. There was nobody there. I went to bed and slept."

In London, Miriam went back to Leslie Flint a few days later, and Kenneth Bannister came through. He said he was free of pain and very happy to be with Madys again. He also asked her to tell Mary that Silver Birch was with her. He said Mary would understand what he meant.

Since her father passed over Mary has carried on the work of the Sanctuary, even though it now takes more of her time than ever. She is determined to keep up the high standards her father set and be a good wife to her husband Chris King and a good mother to her three daughters Madys Ann, Nona, and Jane. The adjustment to complete responsibility wasn't easy, but she has managed it and feels that her father would want it that way.

Her clients include the very rich and the very poor, and she gives them all equal time. Medical doctors consult her about their clients and a noted psychiatrist sends her his more difficult patients. One of the readings of which she is proudest took a young man off drugs and led him to give up his friends who had introduced him to drugs.

Her most dramatic mediumistic adventure took place in a mansion in the best part of Mexico City. Once the property of a wealthy man, it had been converted into an embassy for a central European republic. "I was asked to go to this embassy because it was haunted. They couldn't keep maids or butlers working there. The big sliding doors would bang at night. There were footsteps in the Ambassador's bedroom, and ever since the Ambassadress moved into the house, she had been extremely ill. Every time she walked into the library, she felt someone was trying to choke her. They had called in a priest to exorcise it, but he hadn't done any good. When I went there I headed straight for the library and when I walked in, someone started to choke me! So I said, 'Now look, I'm not a child and I'm not going to be frightened away by such childish things, so stop it!' But I will admit that I brought out a little cross that my guide had given me for just such occasions. My guide at that time was a Catholic priest named Thomas. I took Thomas with me, I can assure you!

"I became aware of a man sitting with his head in his hands on one of the chairs. 'Who are you?' I asked.

" 'Who are *you*?' he replied. 'This is my house. What are you doing in my house?' I told him I had been invited. He said, 'What gives these other people the right to invite strangers into my house? I can communicate with you. Tell them to get out. I don't want strangers in my house.'

"I sat down beside him and asked very calmly what had happened to him.

" 'I was driving my car up the Paseo de la Reforma,' he said, 'and my car hit a tree. I got out of the car when it wouldn't start again and walked home. Ever since then no one has spoken to me. You are the first one. They think they've buried me, but here I am.'

"And I said, 'Can't you see that you've passed to the world of spirit?'

"He said, 'No! I don't want to be in the world of spirit

because my life on earth would probably take me to hell and I haven't had absolution and I didn't make a confession or anything like that.'

"I tried to convince him that he was wasting his time just sitting around there. Then I said, 'I know a priest who can give you absolution. If you receive absolution from him, will you leave this place?' Well, he wasn't so sure. He wanted to talk to his wife before he went away, and I promised to arrange it.

"I went into the hallway and asked the Ambassadress who had owned this house before their government bought it. She told me it was a Mexican industrialist who had been killed when his car hit a tree on the Paseo de la Reforma. She could show me the spot where it happened, if I was interested. Then I contacted my brother Peter in spirit and asked him to bring over the man's wife, who was also in spirit. He said he'd do it the next day.

"The next day I went back to the embassy, and Peter had brought the man's wife. Even in spirit she was pretty angry with him and didn't want to see him because he had given her a terribly hard life with his lies and his unfaithfulness. He told her he was extremely sorry about everything he had done to her and asked her forgiveness. She said she didn't ever want to see him again, but if it would make his transition easier, she would forgive him, and she left.

"Then the most impressive thing happened. Thomas, my spirit guide, came into the room wearing the most magnificent priestly robes. He looked very tall and dignified and this man knelt in front of him. Thomas made the sign of the cross over him and asked him to rise.

"The man came up and thanked the Ambassadress first of all. He said she was the first person who could sense and listen to him. He thanked my guide, and then thanked me. Then he left.

"But his leaving didn't get rid of all the danger in that place. The house was occupied by other evil spirits. This man was not evil, but he had led a dissolute life and had managed to attract several evil entities to him. For some reason, they had kept him earthbound in that house and were feeding off him. They were certainly feeding off the *people* in the house. I knew I couldn't get rid of them all, but I did manage to make a deal with them. I told them that if they would leave the people in the house alone, I would pray for them and help them get back on the right plane. They promised to cooperate. They must have listened to me because the Ambassadress told me that afterward her friends asked her if she had painted the interior of the house—it seemed so much happier and brighter.

Afterward, when the Ambassador and his wife left, they tried to tell the new Ambassador that there was something wrong with the house and how to treat the unseen entities in it. But they didn't listen. Soon after moving into the house they were in a car crash and the wife was killed."

My friend, the writer James Crenshaw, called me as soon as he heard I was making plans to go to Mexico City. "Before you leave Los Angeles," he said, "I want to give you the name and address of a place down there that is unbelievable. It's unique in the entire psychic scene." I listened, because Jim Crenshaw has been reporting the occult world—all over the world—for over twenty years. "It's called the Templo de la Fe," he continued, "and you will see a hundred mediums all in trace at the same time! Don't miss it!" When I tried to get into the inner sanctum of "The Temple of Faith," I found Jim's name a golden key.

"The Temple of Faith" is hardly a temple, it's more like an overcrowded bus station. It sits in the middle of the block at 80 Tolnahuac Street in the San Simon Colony of Mexico City. On the days it is closed to the public, you would walk right by it and not even notice there was a "temple" there, but on Tuesdays and Fridays you'd have to fight your way through the crowds going in or streaming out. Either of those days would be a truly unique experience for the student of the "psychic arts," for he would see thousands of people milling around, talking, drinking blessed water, and waiting to consult one of the almost one hundred mediums who line the walls of this "temple."

The doors open on Tuesday and Friday at seven A.M. and close at seven P.M. During these twelve hours, an estimated eight thousand people go in and out of that building. They go in with fears, problems, illnesses, and needs. It is said that a vast majority of them go out happy, hopeful, and cured. Certainly there is a different expression on the faces that leave the "temple." Most of them are smiling and have a lightness to their walk.

Inside, four specially trained helpers keep the crowd flowing. They make sure the faithful keep in line, that they sit on the brown painted backless benches and that they move immediately when their turn comes to go before a medium. Most of those I saw there were middle-class Mexicans. There were a few of the poorer people there as well as a sprinkling of the upper classes. The crowd seemed evenly divided between men and women, and a number of the latter held tiny babies in their arms or had small children tugging at their skirts.

The mediums stood against or sat on similar wooden benches around three sides of the large hall. Most were women, but there were a few men. The babble of their voices and the rapid movements of their hands made the noise and confusion in the room even greater. They were *all* in trance, all giving counsel, all passing their hands over the faces and bodies of the faithful. They were all advising, prescribing, and healing.

At a back corner near the entrance, a long line of other faithful waited to fill bottles, jars, cans, and plastic gallon jugs with a special blessed water. This water, called "balsam," is charged with super powers. It cures, it calms, it brings good luck, it gives confidence. It also comes straight out of a pipe connected to the city water supply. Outside the "temple" it is ordinary water, but once it comes into the "temple" and spills into the large basin and receives the vibrations of the room, it becomes "balsam." A sign over the spigot warns: "The balsam should be used pure and clean as it is here. Don't put anything in it. Don't sell it because it will lose its powers."

Up front, against the many-times-painted blue wall is a large altar sitting on a raised platform. During the week it is thinly veiled by a transparent yellow and brown striped curtain. There are no statues of Jesus or any of the saints. There are several enormous bouquets of gladiolas surrounding a foot-high round urn where a wick floating in scented oil burns perpetually. In the center of the wall is a large banner with an eye painted in the middle of a yellow triangle. To one side of this platform is a larger-than-life bronze bust of a woman. Someone told me it was the late Señora Pacheco.

The still-living Señor Pacheco will be one hundred years old in 1981. A large man with broad features and thick white curly hair, he was pushed out in a wheelchair to meet me. He had broken his left leg in a fall and it was in a heavy cast. I asked him why his mediums didn't heal the leg, and he smiled. "It is very difficult to mend bones as old as mine. But the healers have removed all the pain. I don't have to take any pills for it. It is inconvenient, but soon I'll be up and around."

Could he tell me something about himself? He shook his head. "I would rather you'd write about the temple. It is my life's work. If anything should speak for my life, it is my temple."

"It is not an ordinary temple, you understand," spoke up a white-haired gentleman, very distinguished in a perfectly tailored gray business suit. "It was founded fifty years ago, in 1927, by Señor Pacheco and his wife. Fifty years of dedicated service to God. Untiring service to those who have problems and need somewhere to go. Fifty years is a long time to dedicate yourself to others."

I agreed and turned back to "the guide of guides," Señor Pacheco. "Is this a Spiritist church like the ones in Brazil?"

"Most definitely not!" he replied. "This is a *Spiritualist* temple. We do not deal with spirits, but rather with the divine and direct intervention of God." He waved a hand at the man in the gray suit. "Read him the page in the pamphlet."

The man took back a yellow printed brochure I'd been given when I first came in, turned to an inner page, and cleared his throat.

"That's all right," I said. "I read Spanish."

He cleared his throat again and began:

" 'When we are asked what religion we are, we reply: we are Marian Trinity Spiritualists.

" 'Question: What do you mean by Spiritualists?

" 'Answer: Spiritualists means that we oppose materialism and that with our acts and thoughts we are preparing the way for those who wish to speak, spirit to spirit, with God our Father.

" 'Question: Why are you Marians?

" 'Answer: We are Marians because we believe in the purity of Blessed Mary, Mother of God and our own mother.

" 'Question: What do you mean by Trinity?

" 'Answer: We are Trinitarians because we believe in the Holy Trinity; God the Father, God the Son, and God the Holy Ghost.

" 'Question: What are the aims of your Spiritualism?

" 'Answer: To bring good to humanity, to eliminate the ego, and do away with fanaticism.' "

"Now I have a question," I said, but Señor Pacheco had turned his wheelchair around and was heading for an open door.

"You will go into the temple with my assistant here and he will tell you everything you need to know. And I want to invite you to my hundredth birthday party in 1981. Will you come?"

I smiled and nodded.

"I'll be looking forward to seeing you again then. My blessings on you, my son," and he wheeled around the doorway and was gone.

To get from Señor Pacheco's private quarters to the front door of the "temple," we had to go outside onto the sidewalk. Gray Suit (who refused to give me his name— "God knows who I am") had seen me taking photos of the myriad street vendors and he made it clear the "temple" had nothing to do with them at all.

"Look at those dried bats!" he exclaimed, "And those love potions, those colored candles and those good luck charms! That isn't *our* doing. We have no control over what is sold here on the public street. It gives the 'temple' a bad image. That garbage is certainly *not* Spiritualism!" Yet in spite of his protestations, many of those going in and out of the "temple" were stopping to look at and buy some of that "garbage." Then I saw three young women fastening skirts around their waists and rolling up the legs of their slacks.

"Why are they doing that?"

"Señor Pacheco has a rule that women are not allowed to come into the temple with bare shoulders or in trousers," Gray Suit replied. "All skirts must be down below the knees. It is his rule and he will not change it."

I thought that the sight of women donning full skirts and rolling up pant legs in front of the "temple" was more detrimental to the "temple's" image than if they had been allowed to go in as they were, but I didn't say it.

I also didn't mention that I had heard how Señor Pacheco got his start. According to one knowledgeable source, back in 1917 José Pacheco was a young revolutionary who fought alongside "First Chief" Venustiano Carranza. When Carranza won and assumed dictatorial powers, he awarded his faithful aide with more than 25 acres of land in San Simon colony. Years later, under "divine inspiration," Pacheco began to sell the property off in commercial and residential lots. With that money he built and has maintained his "Temple of Faith."

I say "maintained" because the services of the "temple" are free! No money changes hands. There are no signs or boxes asking for contributions. The readings and consultations with the mediums are free of charge. The holy water is free. The only thing that one must pay for is a healing with herbs called a *limpia* [cleansing], that takes place in a small smoke-filled room for the token fee of one peso, about twelve cents.

The mediums also work for free. Many of them travel long distances, at their own expense, to go into trance and advise the needy. Many of them are professional people (I was shown one lawyer, three bank clerks, four school teachers, and one registered nurse while I was there) and usually they lose part of their wages while they are attending at the "temple." The mediums work a two-hour shift, and Gray Suit told me over fifteen hundred mediums have been trained in special Monday classes over the past fifty years.

As he led me toward a medium for a reading of my own, he wanted me to understand that these mediums were *not* possessed by spirits but rather were all tuned into "God's divine intelligence." They were speaking the words and thoughts of God, and not the ideas and suggestions of some discarnate entity. Because of this, he explained, you never had to tell a medium what your problem or ailment was. The medium knows why you are there before you even open your mouth.

My medium was a rather corpulent middle-aged woman who was standing next to the altar. I assumed that was a position of authority. She blessed me by pouring some balsam on my hands and asking for protection. Then she started giving a long and rather rambling discourse about searching for the truth and knowing when I had really found the truth. Then there was something about infinite intelligence, the power of the printed word, and the need that all men have that eventually brings them back to God. As she spoke, her special assistant would reach up with a Kleenex and pat the beads of perspiration from her face. She had already had thirty-two clients that morning and still had a half hour to go. I observed her closed eyes, her irregular breathing, and her sweet-smelling breath and wondered just how much good she, and all the others, were really doing.

When my counseling was over and I was back in the audience, I soon found out. "Why are you here?" I asked a young lady.

"I didn't have any ambition. I didn't want to get a job, I didn't get out of bed until almost noon every day. I just didn't have any energy. Then a friend insisted I come to the 'temple.' After just one visit, my energy came back and I took a good paying job. I'm much happier now, and I'm here today because my sister has a bad headache and she needs a healing."

"Why are you here?" I asked a middle-aged well dressed woman.

"When I was a child I was injured and couldn't walk. My parents had me see the best doctors in all Mexico, but there was nothing any of them could do. Then I decided to come here. That was three months ago. Now I am out of my wheelchair and can walk without the aid of a cane. I come here once a week now just to give thanks for the blessings I've received."

"Why are you here?" I asked a man who had three children with him.

"I was laid off from my job and couldn't find another one. I have five children and needed to buy food for them. One day I was desperate and heard about the 'temple' and came here. I'll admit that in the beginning I didn't believe any of it. I'm a Catholic, you understand. Anyway, after coming here just three times, I found a fantastic job. I now have all the money I need for my family and I just bought a new car. I came here today hoping the spirits will help my little boy with his bad eyesight."

"Why are you here?" I asked a woman with a tiny baby in her lap.

"I have been married for seven years and was never able to bear a child. I would always lose them in the third month. My husband wanted a child as badly as I did, and I was afraid that if I didn't conceive he would leave me for another woman who could give him a son. I heard about the 'temple' and came here every week during my last pregnancy. My doctors told me to stay home and rest in bed, but I knew I had to come here. My baby was born two months ago. Thanks to the 'temple' I have given my husband a son."

I had hired a taxi for the entire day and got back into it when I had finished at the "temple." The driver pulled out of the small street and into the mainstream of traffic. "You know," he said to me, "while you were in there, I was thinking. I was trying to define my own definition of *faith*. It's not an easy word to pin down, but I think I have it—at least for myself," he added quickly.

"I'd like to hear it," I said, expecting something straight out of catechism rote.

"To me, faith is a belief that I am not alone and no matter how bad the present is, the future will always be better. I know this to be a fact and it has become my faith.

"You know something else? I think that at one time, years and years ago, man was able to do incredible things with his mind. If a man decided he wanted to be in Paris, France, then in an instant he would be in Paris. Physically be there. You see, I don't think man has progressed at all. Not the way our religious and scientific leaders tell us he has. I think we have *regressed* as human beings. Because we've had to worry about food for our bodies and a place to live, we've used our brains only to acquire material things.

"The mind is a wonderful instrument and it can bring on disease just as it can bring on all the great things in life. I wish our schools would start teaching the kids how to use their minds and not just their brains. There is a difference you know. Do you agree with me, señor? Señor?"

I sat in the back of this battered Mexican taxi in stunned silence.

# Index

"African Genesis" men, 45
Agnosticism of Francisco Madero, 177-78
Alcala, Leonardo, 24-29
Aleman, Miguel, 182
Alscaltingo Vedalgo, 141
Amadou, Robert, 23
Amazon basin, 44, 192
Amulets, 136-41, 198
  belief in, 14
  evil eye as, 121
  hummingbird as, 138
  from Spain, 117, 124
Andes, 43
Apparitions, 14-17
  of Christ, 90-91
  with materialization, 182-86
  of Virgin Mary, 64-74
*Apparitions at Tepeyac: Myth or Reality, The* (Toledano Hernandéz), 69-72
Apports, 199
Aquino, Marcos de, 71
Arauz, Milton, 32-33
Argentina, spiritualism in, 172
Arigo (Brazilian healer), 80
Armadillo skulls as curative, 135-36
Arnica as curative, 134-35
Association of Professors and Investigators (API), 23-24
Astrology, 114, 116, 142-43
Astronomy, 47-50
Atlantis, 46
  *See also* Lemuria
Avila, Jorge, 1-2
Aztecs
  arrival of, 42
  calendar of, 143
  conquest of, *see* Conquest of Mexico
  herbalists of, 131-33
  legends of, 39-50
  medicine of, 135-36
  Nahuatl language of, 46
  psychic life of, 114
  religion of, 108-9
  sacrifices by, 107-8
  temple at Tepeyac of, 71-72
  witches of, 116-89

Badiano, Juan, 132
Bannister, Kenneth, 192-98
  Sanctuary of, 197-202
Barbanell, Maurice, 198
Basiguare, church of, 93
Bering Strait, 42
Bender, Hans, 23
Bertotto Amezcua, María Teresa, 183-84
Black mass, 24
Blessed water, 206
Blood, ritual role of, 107
Body of Christ
  magic mushrooms as, 164
  in Mayan belief, 151
Bones in witchcraft, 124
Bookburning, 149-50
Bound, Robert, 4
Brazil, 106
  gold in, 192
  healers in, 131-32
  spiritualism in, 168, 207
Bustamante, Fray Francisco, 70-71

Cacaloxóchitl, 134
Café Khrishna (Mexico City), 32-38
Café Turco (Mexico City), 31
Calles, Plutarco Elías, 79
Camarena, Jorge González, 71
Carbon-14 test, 43
Card reading, 135
  *See also* Tarot
Cárdenas, Lázaro, 194
Carlos V of Spain, 56-58
Carranza, Venustiano, 209
Castor oil as curative, 135
Catholic Church
  cemeteries of, 3
  churches of, 41
  converts to, 63-64
  devotion to, 173
  failure of dogma of, 9
  healers and, 90
  Inquisition in Mexico by, 119, 188
  intolerance of spiritualism by, 171-75, 183
  intolerance of witchcraft by, 117, 123-24
  pagan temples refurbished by, 72

# INDEX

Catholic Church, *continued*
  priests in, 88
  renunciation of, 6
  response to miracles by, 65-66, 68-69
  saints of, 72
  secularization of ceremony in, 98-105
Cattle, exorcism of, 156-57
Ce Acatl (year 1519), 40
Ceballos, 13-14
C.E.F.F.F.F.A.C. (The Investigating Center for Extraterrestial Spacecraft and Unusual Phenomena, Private Association), 13
Cemeteries
  grave-robbing in, 110-12
  in Latin America, 3
  in Mexico City, 109-12
  of San Augustín Tecómitl, 109
Chaldeans, astronomy of, 48
Chaneques, 6-10
Chichimecas tribe, 42
Chickens as cure, 156
Chihuahua State, 93
Cholula, pyramid at, 41, 56
Chontales, religion of, 114-16
Christ
  belief in, 148
  crucified, 39, 81, 93, 97, 116, 139
  imitation of, 81-82
  infant, dolls and images of, 125-26
  in Quetzalcoatl, 39, 45-46
  Sacred Heart of, 78
  as Tata Dios, 93, 95
  *See also* Jesus
Christianity
  belief in, 148
  in Mexico, 42, 93-94
  paganism and, 70, 92, 138-39
  witchcraft and, 117-18
Church of Satan, 24
Circle of Fidencio, 80
Class struggle, 30
Clifton (Arizona), 76
Coahuila State, 10, 76, 177
*Cochizxihuitl*, 133
Collision of planets, 44
Communion by spiritualists, 185
Conchita the healer, 124-29
Conquest of Mexico, 6, 42, 107, 150, 186
  for gold, 51-61, 71
  smallpox epidemic during, 61-62
  supernatural and, 117
Conquest of Yucatan, 150
  *See also* Cortez Hernando

Constantino, Niño Fidencio Sintora, 76-83
Corn
  as curative, 113
  as divination, 155
  in Mayan diet, 151
  offerings of, 100-2
Corn spirit
  in Mayan belief, 151-52
  rebirth of, 95
Cortez, Hernando, 5, 6, 42, 44, 47, 150
  iconography of, 140
  Moctezuma and, 54-62
Crenshaw, Brenda, 198
Crenshaw, James, 205
Cross, 140, 154-55
  *See also* Crucifix
Crucifix
  of Caravaca, 137
  ritual of, 118, 190-91
Crucifixion of Christ, 39, 81, 93
Cuauhtémoc, visitations of, 186, 188
Cuitlacoche, 113
Cuba, 54, 59
Cuernavaca, 41
*Curanderos, see* Healers
Cusco, 44

Davis, Denny, 134-35
Day of the Dead, 109-12
Dead
  power of, 106-7
  resuscitation of, 144
Deer, spirit of, 157
"De-gravitation" of stones, 43-44
Deluge theories, 49-50
Departed souls returning, 14, 19-23
Devil
  apparitions worked by, 65, 200
  of Chontales Indians, 115-16
  surgical works of, 188
  Tezcatlipoca, 46-47
  witchcraft and, 117
  written works of, 149
  *See also* Satan
Devil fish as curative, 135
Diaz, Bernal, 51-52, 55-56, 71
Diaz, Porfirio, 178-79
Diego, Juan, story of, 63-69
Digitalis, 134
Doña Marina, 55
*Doors of Perception* (Huxley), 165
*Drum and Candle* (St. Clair), 106
Duke University, 23-24
Duplessy, Yvonne, 23

Egypt
  astronomy of, 48

214

# INDEX

Egypt, *continued*
   cultural evolution in, 45
Eisenbud, Jules, 23
"El Crespillo," 71
El Tajun, 41
Elizabeth II (Queen), 196
Espinazo, 76-83
   "Saint of," 81
*Estafiate*, 133
Etheric body, 153
Etheric vibrations, 143, 145-46
Evil eye, 15, 118, 121, 124, 146-47
   *See also* Amulets
Evil spirits, 106, 145, 204-5
Exorcism, 135, 203
Extrasensory experience, 188

Fate, in Mayan belief, 114, 151
Fidencio Sintora Constantino, Niño, 76-83
First Lady of the World (María Engracia), 24-29
"Flesh of the Gods," 164
Flint, Leslie, 201-2
Flood of Ogyges, 49
Ford, Arthur, 198
Fox Sisters, 171
France, spiritualism in, 176
Friar's rhubarb, 134

Garcia Doreste, Salvador, 24
God
   body of, 151
   goodness of, 147
   vision of, 147-48
God Leonardo (Leonardo Alcala), 24-29
God of the Sun, 101, 105
Goddess of the Rain, 101, 105
Gold, 51, 55-61, 192
Gonzalez, Manuel Angel, 7-9
Gran Alcalde, 154
Grave-robbing, 110-12
Green River (Utah), rocket launching at, 13-14
Guadalajara, 15, 149
   Libertad Market in, 140
   spiritualism in, 172
Guanajuato, 176
   mummies of, 1-4
Guatemala, spiritualism in, 176
Gueda, Sara, 123
Guerreo State, 5, 11
Gulf of Mexico, 44
Gustavo (card reader), 32-38
Gutierrez Hernandez, Luis, 140-48

Hallucinogenic mushrooms, 162-70
   *Life* magazine on, 164

Hamer, Madys, 193, 196-97
Hare Khrishna, 24
Haro Lopez, José de, 9
Healers (*curanderos*)
   in Brazil, 131
   with herbs, 206
   in United States, 131
Healings, 14, 32, 124-29, 155
   with chickens, 156
   Christian mystics as, 75-90
   by spiritualists, 184-88
Heaven and hell, Aztec afterlife in, 108-9
Hemp cactus, 78
Herbalists, 130-48
   relationship to witches, 136
Hernandez, Francisco, 134
*History of the Plants of New Spain* (Hernandez), 134
Huautla, 163
Huejotingo Convent, 71
Hueyatlaco, 43
Huichole Indians, 157-61
   Christianity and, 157
   God (Tatewari), 157
*Huihuitzyocochizxihuitl*, 133
Huitzilopochtli, celebration of, 59-60
Human sacrifice, 107-8
Hummingbird as amulet, 139
Hummingbird flower as curative, 133
Hurkos, Peter, 33
Huxley, Aldous, 16

Idolatry, 70-71
Igartua, Ricardo, 123
Illdefonso, Don, 162
*Illustracion Espirita, La*, 172, 176
"Image of the Virgin Mary, The" (Sanches), 70
Incas, use of cocoa leaf by, 133
Institute of Parapsychological Studies (Mexico City), 187
Ipecac, 134

Jalap as curative, 134
Jalapa, 74
Jalisco State, 25
Jesuits, 93
Jesus
   apparitions of, 90-91
   castigated, 79
   as healer, 83, 87-89
   icons of the infant, 125-26
   *See also* Christ
Juarez, Benito, 4
Judas, 95
Judeo-Christian myth, 45

# INDEX

Kardek, Allan, 172
Karma, 146
Kauyamarie (Holy Person Deer), 157
King, Chris, 198
King, Mary, 189-205
Kirlian photography, 23

La Cruz, Juan de, 71
La Luz Bernal, María de, 139
Las Limas, 72-74
Lake Tequesquitengo, 11
Larcher, Marcel, 23
Lawrence of Arabia, 192
Legends, 39-50
Lelo de Larrea, Evangelina Padilla de, 183-86
Lemuria, continent of, 43-44
Leprechauns, 6-10
LeVey, Anton, 24
Levitation, 90
*Life* magazine, 160
*Limpia*, defined, 210
Lopez, Abel, 8
Lopez, Monica, 83-91
Lopez de la Fuente, Enrique, 77-79
Lopez de Pantoja, Ramón and Pilar, 4
Lord's Prayer said before spiritualist session, 185
Los Mochis, 11
Los Santos Monteil, Carlos de, 11
Love potions, 137
Lovette, John, 199
LSD, 161
Luisito, 182-86

Madero, Francisco, 73-75, 77
Magic, 29, 135
Malaria, cure for, 135
Manzanilla, curative powers of, 135
Marian Trinity Spiritualists, 208
Marijuana, 165
Mars, cosmology of, 48-49
Martiny, Marcel, 23
Materialization by spiritualists, 182-86
Mayans, 47, 62, 107
    corn and, 151
    cosmology of, 152
    libraries of, 149
    spiritualism of, 151-52
    witchcraft of, 117
Mayflowers as curative, 133
Mayo Indians, 76
Maximillian (Emperor), 4, 193
Mechoacan, 134
Medals, *see* Amulets
*Mediums Book, The*, 172
Mediums, *see* Spiritualists
Mendoza, María 113-14

Metaphysical beliefs, 19-29
Mexican-American War, 131
Mexican Association of the Friends of Tibet, 24
Mexican Association of Parapsychological Investigators (AMIP), 23-24
Mexico City (ancient) (Tenochtitlán), Spanish conquest of, 51-62
Mexico City (modern), 4-5, 19-38, 79, 82, 203
    Anthropology Museum in, 44
    British Embassy in, 5
    Institute of Parapsychology Studies in, 187
    International Airport at, 11-13
    National History Museum in, 9, 101
    National Pawnshop in, 87
    1911 earthquake in, 179-80
    Plaza de Tres Cultures in, 5
    racism in, 30-31
    San Angel district in, 22, 195
    San Simon Colony in, 109, 205
    Sonora Market in, 135, 138
    spiritualism in, 171-72, 175, 201-8
    subway lines in, 4
    Templo de la Fe in, 205-12
    Tepeyac hill, 63-72
    Tlateloco, 4, 5
    United States Embassy in, 162-63
    Xochimilco section of, 36
    Zona Rosa section of, 32
Michoacan State, 96
Miracles, 79, 83-90, 155
"Miraculous hummingbird," 138-39
Mixtecs, 62
Moctezuma, 51-62
Montero Lagunes, Cirila, 7
Mummification, 125
    in Guanajuato Municipal Cemetery, 1-4
Murillo, Bartolomé Esteban, 71

Nahuatl language, 46, 55, 63-4, 132
Nahuatlacas tribes, 42
NASA (National Aeronautics and Space Administration), 13-14
National University of Mexico, 9
Nayarit State, 157
Niño Fidencio, 76-83
*Noche Triste, La*, 61
Nogales (Arizona), 76
Nuevo Leon State, 76, 79

Oaxaca (city), 149
Oaxaca State, 31, 44, 110, 114-15, 162, 167
*Objectos Volantes no Identificados*

# INDEX

*Objectos Volantes, continued*
(OVNIS) (UFOs), 10-14
Occult happenings, 14, 19
Olmec culture, 44, 73-74
Ortiz de la Huerta, Carlos, 184
Osiris seed, 138

Pacheco, José, 207-12
Pachita, 186-88
Paranormal experience, 14, 188
Parapsychology, 23
Pelletier, S.A., 11
Peru, 43
Piranha jaw as curative, 132
Plants, curative powers of, 131-45
Poltergeists, 23
Popocatepetl, 12
Popovitch, Alex and Marie, 193-94
Portillo Zaragoza, Carmen, story of, 176-78
Portland Cement Manufacturing Company (Tolteca), 193
Powders for healing, 136-37
Prophecy, 114
Psilocybe mushrooms (*Psilocybe mexicana*), 158-66
Psychic arts, 206
*See also* Spiritualists
*Psychic News*, 198
Psychic phenomena, 14, 19
social class and, 30-31
*Psychic World of California, The*, 43
Psychics, 32, 114
Psychokinesis, 23
Puebla, 149
Huejotingo Convent in, 71
Puebla State, 141
Pulque, 46
Pyramid of the Sun and Moon, 40, 42, 55

Quetzalcoatl
compared to Christ, 39, 45-46
legends of, 14, 39-62
overthrown by Tezcatlipoca, 108
pyramid to, 56
Temple of, 40-41
as Venus, 46-48
Quinine, 134

Rafael, 71
Rebellion of 1891, 76
Refugio, Gonzalez, General, 176
Refugio, Moises, 176
Religion
a healer's view of, 148
iconography of, 140
Sufi, 24

Religion, *continued*
*See also* Catholic Church; Christianity; God
Revolution of 1919, 30
*Revue Espírite, La*, 172, 173, 177
Reynault, Colonel, 193
Rheumatism, curatives for, 142
Roll, William, 24
Romans, astronomy of, 48
Rue as curative, 135

Sabina, María, 163-70
Sacrifice
of prisoners, 45, 53, 58, 107-8
of Quetzalcoatl, 50
Sahagún, Fray Bernardino de, 57-58, 70
St. Francis, 87
St. John the Baptist, festival of, 97-105
Salazar, Severiano and Rosita, 72-74
Saltillo, 10
Salt Lake (Utah), 44
San Agustín Tecómitl, cemetery of, 109
San Angel, 55, 195
San Luis Potosí, 10, 113
San Simon colony, 209
Sanches, Benigno, 172
Sanches, Manuel, 70
Sanchez Perez, Juan M., 24
Sanctuary of Kenneth Bannister, 197-202
Santo Domingo, 54
Sasparilla, curative power of, 134
Satan, 24
"books of," 150
*See also* Devil
Scopolamine, 133
Seabra, Roberto, 180
Seances, 182
*See also* Spiritualism
Seers, *see* Shamans
Shamans
among Huichole, 157
among Zinacantecos, 153-57
Sierra Madre mountains, 76, 93
Sinaloa State, 11, 75
Skulls, symbolism of, 109-10
Sky-earth in Mayan cosmology, 152
Smallpox epidemic in Tenochtitlan, 61-62
Sorcerers, 107
*See also* Witches
Spain, spiritualism in, 172
"Spirit Works" (quoted), 173-76
Spirit World, 14, 92-93, 106, 115, 203
"Spiritual Blood," 136

# INDEX

Spiritualists
    alliance of, 171-88
    consulted by doctors, 202
    materialization by, 182
    taboo of suicide among, 175-76
Star of David, 140
Sufi religion, 24
Suicide, 175-76
Sun, sacrifice to, 108
Swastika, 140

Tabardillo, 133
Taft, William Howard, 179
Talewari ("Grandfather Fire"), 161
Tarahumara Indians, 93-95
Tarascans, 62, 96-105
Tarot, 14, 31-38, 117, 124
    *See also* Card reading
Tata Dios, 93, 95
Teeth, dreams of, 122-23
Telepathy, 23
Temple of Quetzalcoatl, 40-41
Templo de la Fe, 205-12
Tenochtitlán (ancient Mexico City), 53
Tenotzin, 71-72
Teonanacatl, *see* Psilocybe mushrooms
Teotihuacan
    arrival of Aztecs in, 42
    pyramids at, 40
Tepeyac, hill of, 63-72
Tezcatlipoca, 46, 108, 116
*Tlahcolpahtli*, 132
Tlascalan Indians, 59
Tlateloco, 4, 5, 64, 67
*Tlatlacotic* root, 133
Tlaxcala, 56-57
Tocquet, Robert, 23
Toledano Hernandéz, Manuel, 69-72
Tollan, 42
Tolteca, 193
Toltecs, 39, 41-42, 45
Torreon, 10
Totonacs, 56, 58-59
Transcendental Meditation, 24
Trevino Becerra, Carlos, 24
Trinity, 209
*True History of the Conquest of New Spain, The* (Diaz), 71
Tule bulbs, 136
Twelve Stations of the Cross, 94, 97

UFOs, 10-14
University of Mexico City, 23-24
Urrea, Teresa, 75-76
Uruapan, 95-96

Valerian as tranquilizer, 135
Van der Castle, Dr., 23
Vanilla as curative, 133
Velasquez, Diego, 54
Velikovsky, Immanuel, 48-49
Venus (planet)
    Quetzalcoatl as, 46-48
    worship of, 48, 50
Veracruz, 58-59
Veracruz State, 6, 8, 25
Villa, Pancho, 174-75
Virgin Mary, 64, 70, 71, 93, 97, 186, 204
Virgin of Guadalupe, story of, 63, 72
Virgin of Las Limas, story of, 72-74
Vivanco, Gladys, 123
Von Braun, Wernher, 13-14
Von Wernich, 77-78

Wasson, Gordon, 163
Weeping Ghost, The, 4-5
Wilson, Henry, 179
Witches, 130
    Aztec, 116-19
    god of, 46, 108, 116
    habitat of, 31
    hiring of, 107, 136, 112-21
    Mayan, 121
    patron saint of, 116
    relationship to herbalists, 136
    spirit knowledge of, 146
Witchcraft
    among Aztecs, 116-19
    bones in, 124
    in colonial Mexico, 119-21
    eggs in, 124, 126-29
    spells of, 146
    teeth in, 121-23
"Witches' Powder," 136
*Worlds in Collision* (Velikovsky), 48-49

Xochicalco, 41

Yaqui Indians, 76
Yin-Yang, 140
*Yolloxóchitl* tea, 133
Yolosoche flower, 135
Yucatan, 47, 54-55, 78, 149
    conquest of, 150

Zapata, Emiliano, 131, 178-79
Zapotecs, 62
Zinacantecos, 153-55
Zumarraga, Fray Juan de, 65-71